Books in print and eBook by the author

Sparks of Grace - God Transforms The World With His Grace

Sparks of Grace Volume II - Stories, Essays And Reflections That Touch The Heart and Soul

The WORD Is With Us - God Is With Us As He Transforms The World With His Grace

the WORD is with us

GOD IS WITH US
AS HE TRANSFORMS
THE WORLD WITH
HIS GRACE

JUAN P. AQUINO

WESTBOW
PRESS®
A DIVISION OF THOMAS NELSON
& ZONDERVAN

This book is a work of non-fiction. Unless otherwise noted, the author and the publisher make no explicit guarantees as to the accuracy of the information contained in this book and in some cases, names of people and places have been altered to protect their privacy.

WestBow Press books may be ordered through booksellers or by contacting:

WestBow Press
A Division of Thomas Nelson & Zondervan
1663 Liberty Drive
Bloomington, IN 47403
www.westbowpress.com
844-714-3454

Because of the dynamic nature of the Internet, any web addresses or links contained in this book may have changed since publication and may no longer be valid. The views expressed in this work are solely those of the author and do not necessarily reflect the views of the publisher, and the publisher hereby disclaims any responsibility for them.

Any people depicted in stock imagery provided by Getty Images are models, and such images are being used for illustrative purposes only. Certain stock imagery © Getty Images.

Scripture quotations are taken from The New American Standard Bible®, Copyright © 1960, 1962, 1963, 1968, 1971, 1972, 1973, 1975, 1977, 1995 by The Lockman Foundation. Used by permission.

ISBN: 979-8-3850-2721-7 (sc)
ISBN: 979-8-3850-2722-4 (e)

Library of Congress Control Number: 2024912002

Print information available on the last page.

WestBow Press rev. date: 6/19/2024

Contents

Preface

At my first full-time paying employment right out of college, a friend at the company where I worked as an accountant gave me a beautiful handy notebook as a birthday gift. I was starting to explore my passion for writing, unsure of where it would lead me. The notebook was a mystery, a beautiful enigma. I wondered what in the world I could use it for. It was different from one of those notebooks you have in college. It looked more helpful in writing a love letter or a poem. The notebook was just too beautiful for storing phone numbers or addresses. I wondered if she wanted me to write a love letter or poem. So, I kept it as a souvenir, a token of a potential creative journey.

A serendipitous moment occurred for me in the 1970s when cell phones and laptops were yet to become household names. In a simple yet profound suggestion, my friend proposed that I use the notebook to pen my thoughts about my birthday, friends, or life. Her suggestion was like a spark of grace in the dark, igniting a fire of possibilities. Little did I know this seemingly innocuous advice would catalyze a transformative journey. I began to explore new ideas, capturing anything that piqued my interest, be it love quotes, poems, or famous sayings. The notebook metamorphosed into a personal journal, a portal to my creative odyssey.

Once a blank canvas, the notebook began to fill with a diverse array of content. One-liners and short, funny quotes from famous and not-so-famous people adorned its pages: from poets like Robert Frost, captains of industry such as Henry Ford, philosophers like Socrates, rulers of nations like Nelson Mandela, presidents like Abraham Lincoln, writers like William Shakespeare, movie actors like Charlie Chaplin, cops, comedians, artists, street people, homeless people, etc. Reflections about God, my faith, and anything about life. Personal prayers, too. Ah, yes, notes about saints and holy people, too. Looking back, I realize this was the beginning of my adventure into the world of lore, my interest in discovering the unknown wonders of creative writing.

As I reflect on that significant birthday, my 21st, I am filled with profound gratitude towards my friend. With a single gift, she kindled a passion within me that continues to burn brightly. Her thoughtful gesture set me on a path of self-discovery and creativity, for which I am eternally grateful. Her gift was not just a notebook but a key that unlocked a world of possibilities, and for that, I am forever indebted to her. I can't thank her enough for the profound impact she has had on my life.

Introduction

My personal notes, stories, essays, and reflections are seamless adventures in my writing world. A lot of them found their way in the pages of this book. This book covers people, friendship, faith, spirituality, love, life, God and the Good News of salvation. It also further explores the unknown space of signs and wonders that are only possible by the grace of God.

The Word Is With Us is a courageous dive into the boundless sea of mysteries and narratives that only God, the ultimate and Divine Transformer, can fathom. It unveils the identity of the *Word*, offering a lens to explore thoughts about Jesus Christ, our faith, and life. This book is a gateway to a world of parables, stories, and the Good News that have the potential to revolutionize our minds and hearts, awakening our awareness and inviting our active participation.

The WORD Is With Us illuminates how our unique gifts and blessings can serve as conduits to bring Christ to the world, glorify God, and deepen our gratitude to the Almighty Father. This book is not just a guide but a catalyst, empowering us to appreciate and act on our potential to be a transformative part of the Word's impact on the world.

Part One directs our attention to the power of our thoughts, which mysteriously evolve into insights and learning experiences, guiding our journey with Christ. Our thoughts, when articulated, take the form of stories unique to each of us that we can share with others. These stories, filled with hope, have the potential to inspire others to venture out into the world, embrace it, and share the Good News.

Part Two attempts to search our hearts and find consolation in the Word's presence at every moment. We hope that God's Word present in us will find its way into the hearts, minds, and souls of others, including those who are about to be lost.

Part Three attempts to express the words of wisdom and understanding from the Holy Spirit into our hearts with the hope that someone may retain them. I hope those words reach not only our hearts, but also our minds and souls. The Word conveys words of wisdom into our hearts so that they may reside within our whole being, not only for the betterment of ourselves but also of others.

Part Four offers a lens to discover what lies beyond God's gifts of wisdom and our thoughts of God's grace. It allows us to find out who He is, He who called us in the first place, so that we may cling to Him. God calls us to tell the story of our redemption by Him and how our lives are transformed by Him as He transforms the entire world. God calls us to share with others all the blessings, gifts, signs, and wonders we have seen, felt, received, tasted, and experienced in Him, with Him, and through Him.

After Part One of the book, each chapter is meticulously titled with a Gospel Reading and the corresponding Scripture citation (except Chapters 1 and 2 of Part Three). These titles, painstakingly crafted, are not mere labels but profound interpretations or reflections of the Scripture reading. I earnestly hope and pray they reflect the profound spirit under which they were written, nothing less.

As written in this book, the Gospels are laid out in the same order and chronology as in the Bible, i.e., Matthew, Mark, Luke, and John. Also included, where appropriate, are the specific Gospel Parallel citation/s applicable to the primary Gospel. These Gospel Parallel citations are not mere references, but they are included to draw the reader's attention to the Evangelists who may have written their version of the same Gospel, thereby enriching the reader's understanding of the Gospel's context and authorship. This addition will help students, sisters, brothers in the faith, and other interested readers during their studies, reflections, and prayer. These Gospel Parallel or Parallels follow immediately after the primary Gospel citation, indicated by a GP*.

The Table of Contents is not just a summary but a reliable guide for the reader searching for those Gospel Parallels—GP's at a glance of some sort. In the Table of Contents and all of the Parts or Chapters of this book, the primary gospel citation, when applicable, is highlighted, followed by the GP citations, if applicable. Rest assured, the Table of

Contents is a trustworthy companion in your journey through the Gospels.

I hope this book will deepen your reflections and appreciation of God's eternal love for us. In that spirit, at the end of each chapter, you will see a prayer. Our prayers and hope will drive us to Christ, and the Holy Spirit will enlighten us.

Just as I know deep in my heart that I will always return to this book and use it as a source of prayer, my wish and hope will always be that it will serve the same purpose for you. In that way, we may have the peace and love which the Lord always desires for us to have.

Let us pray:

God our Father, "Emmanuel" God with us, You who transforms the world with your Love, You who gives Wisdom and Hope, your Word brings the riches of your grace in every moment of our lives. Let your Word be a lamp to guide us. May your Holy Spirit direct our minds and our lips. With a contrite heart and a humble spirit, we lift up our hearts and souls to You. Give us the courage and strength to proclaim your glory and sing your praises always. Animate us so that with your Word, our actions may become worthy of your plans for us. Help us in all our weaknesses so that whatever we say and do will be more pleasing to You. You are the fountain and source of all grace and salvation. Renew us in your grace. Remain with us and may your grace be a sun that never sets. May the word of Christ dwell among us in all its richness. Father, into thy hands, we commend our spirit.

We ask all these through your Son, our Lord Jesus Christ, who lives and reigns with You and the Holy Spirit, God, for ever and ever. Amen.

GP* = Gospel Parallel or Parallels

Feast of The Visitation of the Blessed Virgin Mary
May 31, 2024

PART ONE

THOUGHTS ARE TRANSFORMED
INTO WORDS AND AMAZING STORIES

*"Do not conform yourself to this age but be transformed by
the renewal of your mind, that you may discern what is the
will of God, what is good and pleasing and perfect."*
– Romans 12:2

Have you ever experienced the sheer joy when words and unique
thoughts, with their beauty and splendor, effortlessly flow from you?
These moments, whether they occur during a conversation with a friend
or while jotting down notes, are what some call 'inspired '. I prefer to
think of them as special and graced moments, a pure delight of writing.
Be transformed by the renewal of your mind.

Have you ever felt that sudden surge of inspiration to write? If you
have, don't let it slip away! It's an adventure waiting to unfold. You'll
be amazed at the unexpected turns your words might take. Even if the
words don't come, let the anticipation linger. That very air, pregnant
with possibilities, silent but rich with subdued joy will guide you. And
before you know it, you'll be onto something extraordinary.

Find a good place to write—somewhere quiet. It would help if you
had quality time. My best writing times are usually very early in the
morning, even before the roosters signal the crack of dawn with their
beautiful noise. The best thoughts or ideas come when I wake up from

a good night's rest. I grab a pen and paper and jot down a thought or idea—even something that I thought was from a silly dream.

The results will surprise you. Whatever goes down on paper might be that sterling moment. Keep that slip of paper. And when that thought comes back to you, seize the moment! Look at that slip of paper. Expound on it.

Amazing how the mind works. Creativity finds itself.

Prayer: *Almighty God, help me to bring glory to you. Grant me your grace so I may proclaim your Word unceasingly to others. Transform my heart and mind so I may always discern your will. May the word of Christ dwell in me in all its richness. Amen.*

CHAPTER 1

Let The Adventure Begin

"Thus says the LORD who made the earth and gave it form and
firmness, whose name is LORD: Call to me, and I will answer you;
I will tell to you things great beyond reach of your knowledge."
– Jeremiah 33:2-3

By nature, we are explorers. When it comes to writing, there must be something in that world that many people devote their entire lives to. Discovering something that the heart and mind see for the first time makes us realize the beauty and splendor of creation. So why not explore its wonders? Write about it. Discover the mystery of writing for one. Writing projects the mind into the world of the unknown. I followed a dear friend's inspiration and lead. That instinct turned out to be good. I overcame my fears and harnessed every ounce of courage I could muster, a crucial step in my journey.

Even a small dose of courage can lead to great things. When you heed the call of your heart, it can propel you towards unexplored horizons. In the depths of my heart, I was struck by inspiration one day, leading me to pen the following from T.S. Eliot's renowned lines in the *V section, No. 4* of *'Four Quarters' of Little Giddings:*

> *"With the drawing of this Love and the voice of this Calling*
> *We shall not cease from exploration*
> *And the end of all our exploring*
> *Will be to arrive where we started*
> *And know the place for the first time."*[1]

My creative process was a collaborative effort, often sparked during the early hours of the morning when my wife and I would engage in our Morning Prayers. These moments, sometimes before or after dawn or during Evening Prayers, were ripe with profound thoughts that I would eagerly note down, not overthinking, but capturing the essence of what could be in a book or memoir.

My creative journey began with a simple task-brainstorming potential book titles. I would meticulously jot down intriguing, humorous, or even whimsical one-liners that popped into my head. At this stage, my ideas had no connection to religion, spirituality, or the Church. They were playful and diverse, ranging from The Obedient Fool to The King That Needs Tweaking. Other titles perhaps worthy of note here were The Crazy Bug Got Lost in the Dumps, The Firefly That Can Not Fly and Jonah Landed On A Giant Seashell. Little did I know these seemingly unrelated musings would later evolve into profound reflections on my spiritual path. Stay tuned. There could be more.

At the time, publishing a book was the furthest thing from my mind. I was playing with the ideas that were bubbling up in my mind. The thought of me, a published author? It seemed laughable. Yet, I did not discard my notes from reading and writing about quotes from notable figures. I was hungry to uncover new thoughts and ideas that could enrich my journey. I remember one particular day when I stumbled upon a quote that perfectly encapsulated a thought I had been wrestling with. It was a moment of clarity and inspiration that I will never forget, a moment that fueled my determination to continue on this creative path.

I bought new, used, bargain books, no matter what. I visited libraries, garage sales, and flea markets. When I saw books I liked, I bought them for a few cents or a dollar each. Soon, I was overwhelmed! If I wanted to look for a book I knew I had just bought, I could not find it! So, the great sifting began. I started organizing my books based on themes, genres, and authors. The books that did not resonate with me or fit into my current creative journey ended up in a box destined for donation to the local library, where they took them with open hearts for sharing with other people. This struggle with organization was a testament to my passion for knowledge and my determination to find the right sources of inspiration.

But before anything else, I believe putting ourselves in God's presence is always a source of strength and inspiration. With God's help, as we embark on our hopeful and unceasing exploration and discovery of the Word and the Word of God in our midst, let us strive to seek the *"end of all our exploring"*[2] and to *"know the place for the first time."*[3] This spiritual journey is not just mine, but one that we can all embark on together, finding solace and inspiration in our shared faith. Let our adventure begin!

The Scripture texts used in this work are taken from the Saint Joseph Edition of the *New American Bible*. These texts were chosen for their relevance to my journey and the insights they offer. They serve as a guiding light, illuminating my path and deepening my understanding of my experiences. Catholic Book Publishing Co., New York, NY. 1992. Prayers and scripture texts, as indicated, are also taken from the *Saint Joseph Guide for Christian Prayer (The Liturgy of the Hours)* Catholic Book Publishing Corp., New Jersey, NJ, 1970. *catholicbookpublishing. com;* Catechism of the Catholic Church with Modifications from the Editio Typica. Image Book Doubleday, New York, NY. 1994.

Prayer: *Good and loving God, your creation's wonders continually amaze us. You have given us all that we need to help bring this world into your likeness and image. But sometimes, our weakness prevails. Please give us the will and strength to carry on our tasks always. Amen.*

CHAPTER 2

Stories Are Meant To Be Shared

*"You are our letter, written on our hearts, known and read
by all, shown to be a letter of Christ administered by us,
written not in ink but by the Spirit of the living God, not on
tablets of stone but on tablets that are hearts of flesh."*
– 2 Corinthians 3:2-3

Our personal stories, etched on the tablets of our hearts, hold a transformative power. They are not just narratives of our lives but a means to connect with the Spirit of the living God, who authored them within us. Let us not merely taste and savor the great works of writers, poets, philosophers, or people of God, but let us retell them, for in doing so, we can contribute to a world where harmony thrives. This is when we truly appreciate how these great works have profoundly shaped our lives and the lives of others. This is when we can give back and return the graces God has blessed us all.

Isn't this the only way we can see the hope God wants us to have instead of doubt, despair, and death? Isn't this how God wants us to experience His great love and compassion for all? Each one of us has a story to tell. Our lives are, in fact, a story that has already begun the moment we are born. Each one of us is a living book. It is a unique book because while it has a beginning, even when the book physically ends, its stories do not end but continue to live. Such is the power of our lives in the Spirit. Let us embrace this power and share our stories, for they are not just ours but part of a larger, divine narrative.

Our personal stories may be short but they are filled with richness and depth. Though temporary in the grand scheme of things, each of our individual life stories can fill many books with their chapters and sub-chapters. This abundance of stories, this tapestry of experiences, makes life surprisingly joyful. It is a life that is not bound by rigid plans or expectations, but one that is guided by the grace of God, filled with unexpected twists and turns that lead to growth and fulfillment.

There are stories for anyone to appreciate. Stories to be read, heard, and shared. There are moments to enjoy with gratitude for the Lord in His stories. Those stories can be inspiring, with a prayerful, inquiring mind and heart. They have the power to guide us, to help us navigate the challenges and darkness that we may face without real awareness. Your story, no matter how big or small, has the potential to inspire and guide others, to make a profound difference in their lives.

But sometimes, one problem is that we have become so accustomed to how we live our daily lives that we pay little attention to anything that makes life exciting or challenging: following His will. Sometimes, we ignore the wonder and uniqueness of stories given us as gifts in the continuing saga of God's creation and beauty. This 'continuing saga' refers to the ongoing process of God's creation and the beauty that is constantly being revealed in the world around us.

Even when a nagging thought of relevance exists, the storyteller must explore a story. Even if that moment begs for a pause in our busy lives, the story is still worth telling. We tend to ignore those things that do not suit our fancy. We have 'too many minds,' meaning we often have conflicting thoughts and distractions that prevent us from fully engaging with a story. We get distracted.

Distractions in our lives are in themselves stories. They are the narratives that play out when we lose focus or get sidetracked. Sometimes, they are a treasure trove of funny stories, like the time I got lost in a foreign city because I was too busy taking pictures. Some stories could make or break our lives, and others joyful and fruitful. That means we can turn those distractions into something better. They can become lessons and inspirations, guiding us towards a more enlightened path. They can be catalysts in transforming the world with God's help— stories worth considering.

Prayer: *Lord Jesus, you gave us your stories that are now in our hearts and minds. Please help us to understand them better. May your words dwell among us in all their richness. Grant us the grace to use them for your greater glory and the benefit of our souls. Amen.*

CHAPTER 3

Everybody Has A Story

"All these things Jesus spoke to the crowds in parables. He spoke to them only in parables, to fulfill what had been said through the prophet: 'I will open my mouth in parables, I will announce what has lain hidden from the foundation [of the world].'"
– Matthew 13:34-35

Storytelling, a universal language, is a tool Jesus Christ used to teach us. His parables, each word transformative, ingrained the power of stories in our lives. Without stories, life can become monotonous and uneventful. Stories, with their ability to prompt and inspire, are essential for our mental stimulation and growth.

Stories, more than mere narratives, have the power to uplift our spirits and breathe life into our souls. They transcend the boundaries of words and become prayers, touching and animating not just our souls but also those of others.

We love reading stories. Our eyes feast on stories that suit our good senses. We rejoice. We are grateful. If a story is not read, what good is it? *"The unread story is not a story; it is little black marks on wood pulp. The reader reading it makes it live: a thing, a story. – Ursula K. Le Guin."*

We love listening to stories. When someone tells a delightful story, we are all ears. Especially if the story is from a loved one; their stories become our stories. Their stories can transform us.

We love telling stories. Anyone can tell a story, and we can be inspired to tell one or many stories. Anything can be a story, including ourselves. A story can change us. What good is it if a good story is not told or shared? It is next to nothing. Like salt that has lost its flavor.

We love sharing stories with others. We rejoice when we know people are enjoying our stories. Our stories connect us. Friendships are born when stories are shared. There is affinity when a story is shared. Affinity creates intimacy. That is why we are all storytellers. We are natural-born storytellers.

Most of us genuinely believe that storytelling has the power to change lives. Stories inspire people to live better lives. Even just one story can be a survival guide for the many. If someone is facing a struggle of some sort, a story can significantly impact a person's life.

Storytellers are not just conveyors of tales, they are thinkers, peacemakers, healers, and saviors. Stories keep us alive. Stories inspire us. Something we all can cherish. The more storytellers and thinkers, the more people will be inspired, saved, or helped. The more peacemakers and healers, the more people will be taught and appreciate the beauty of creation. Then, more people will learn the lessons of life and even death. Then, more people will smile, laugh, dance, and even cry with joy on their faces. Each storyteller has the power to make a difference, to inspire, and to heal.

Prayer: *Lord Jesus, you opened our hearts, minds, and souls through parables. May your words dwell among us in all their richness. Through them and your grace, you revealed their truths. Enable us always to use them for your greater glory and the benefit of our souls. Amen.*

CHAPTER 4

We Can Be Audacious, Brave, And Steadfast In Our Faith

*"He said to them, 'Because of your little faith. Amen, I say
to you, if you have faith the size of a mustard seed, you
will say to this mountain, 'Move from here to there,' and
it will move. Nothing will be impossible for you.'"*
– Matthew 17:20

A skilled storyteller possesses the unique ability to perceive the unfolding of events in the present, infusing them with life and beauty. Their creative minds extend beyond the realm of the ordinary, envisioning the future. This creativity, akin to the prophets of old and new, allows life to triumph in the Spirit. They achieve what appears impossible, guided solely by faith in their hearts and minds.

Every aspect of our lives, even the seemingly mundane, harbors a story yearning to be heard. The ordinary, upon closer inspection, can transform into the extraordinary. So, why not immortalize these narratives on paper or in the *digital realm,* for yourself or future generations to explore, uncover, or even challenge? You'll be amazed at the heights you can reach.

Expressing and embodying the essence of the Spirit demands fortitude and exceptional courage. It necessitates effort. Yet, the prophets of old, with their abundance of inspiring words and exhortations, propel us into action. They urge us to remain unwavering in our faith.

When Moses was approaching an advanced age and could no longer move freely, the Lord told him not to cross the Jordan. Moses said these words to all of Israel: *"It is the Lord, your God, who will cross before you… Be brave and steadfast; have no fear or dread of them, for it is the Lord, your God, who marches with you; he will never fail or forsake you."* - Deuteronomy 31: 3, 6.

Moses repeated these words when he called Joshua and, in the presence of all Israel, said to him: …" *It is the Lord who marches before you; he will be with you and will never fail you or forsake you. So do not fear or be dismayed." Deuteronomy 31:7.*

After Moses died, the Lord said to Joshua:…*I will be with you as I with Moses: I will not leave you nor forsake you. Be firm and steadfast so that you may give this people possession of the land which I swore to their fathers I would give them. Above all be firm and steadfast, taking care to observe the entire law which my servant Moses enjoined on you….I command you: be firm and steadfast! Do not fear nor be dismayed, for the Lord, your God, is with you wherever you go."* - Joshua 1: 1-9.

In the 18th and 19th chapter of 1 Chronicles, the Lord made David victorious in all his campaigns against his enemies. *(cf 1 Chronicles 18).* In command of David's army, Joab assured his brother Abishai that if the Ammonites would prove more potent than them, he, Joab, would save them. *"Hold steadfast and let us show ourselves courageous for the sake of our people and the cities of our God…".*- 1 Chronicles 19:13.

"Be brave and steadfast; do not fear or lose heart."- 1 Chronicles 22:13.

"…Azariah, son of Oded, came the Spirit of God. He went forth to meet Asa and said to him: Hear me, Asa and all Judah and Benjamin! The Lord is with you when you are with him, and if you seek him he will be present to you; but if you abandon him, he will abandon you. …But as for you, be strong and do not relax, for your work shall be rewarded." – 2 Chronicles 15:1-2; 7.

A good storyteller can be audacious and courageous in the Spirit. When God said to Jeremiah that He had appointed him a Prophet, Jeremiah responded:

"Lord God I know not how to speak; I am too young."- Jeremiah 1:5.

The Lord answered him:

"*Say not, 'I am too young. To whomever I send you, you shall go; whatever I command you, you shall speak. Have no fear before them because I am with you to deliver you." (Jeremiah: 1:7).*

"*Then the Lord extended his hand and touched my mouth, saying, 'See, I placed words in your mouth.'" (Jeremiah 1:4–9)*

These inspiring words hold the potential to bridge the gap between our thoughts and the eternal. They are like divine sparks, waiting to be received by the tiny cells in our brain. Have you ever contemplated this spiritual process? Can you fathom how the brain processes these thoughts, transmuting them into words? This spiritual journey, this transformation of thought into word, is a testament to the profound influence of the Spirit in our lives.

It is amazing how the tiny cells in our brains work! In layperson's terms, the mind forms them into words that the mouth can express. It's not a scientific way to describe how the words find their way into the mouth. But let us leave it at that. Our minds and hearts, with their immense power, have a profound way of enabling thoughts to become meaningful words and actions of the Spirit. But all these can only be possible with the help of the Spirit. I can tell you with lots of certainty that many of those thoughts found their way into the pages of this book!

Prayer: *Father, let your Word be a lamp to guide our feet to follow You. Make our lives triumphant in your Spirit, and keep the wisdom and love You have revealed in your Son before us. May the word of Christ dwell among us in all its richness. Help us to be like Christ in word and deed, for He lives and reigns with You and the Holy Spirit, God, forever and ever. Amen.*

CHAPTER 5

The WORD And The World In Parables

"He spoke to them only in parables, to fulfill what has been said through the prophets: 'I will open my mouth in parables, I will announce what has lain hidden from the foundation[of the world].'"
– Matthew 13:35

The word *parable* is derived from the Greek word *parabole*, meaning an analogy or an illustration. In ancient Greek literature, the word connotes a "moving side by side" or could be used as a "not-so-direct way" of teaching a concept. The story itself could be a model or in the form of an analogy or an example. This oblique way of storytelling was fascinating to many of its followers. In today's world, particularly during a less formal conversation, we usually say "for example," followed by a statement of words, a short story, or an illustration to clarify the intended lesson.

Parables are amazing stories used to clarify or explain a subject more pointedly. During Jesus' time, parables were used as a teaching tool by a *rabbi* (master) or a teacher of the faith. Even as a Divine Teacher, Jesus used parables in His teachings. His listeners were amazed at His teachings. Yet, people did not learn things from Jesus. They heard amazing things from Him and were attracted by His teachings' power and depth. Unbeknownst to them, they tended to cling to Him.

Our Lord used many parables that would become the highlight of His teachings and, to many, the much sought-after stories in the

Christian world. Jesus' parables were not just stories, they were mirrors reflecting our daily lives, our struggles, and our triumphs. He told stories in the context of daily life, reflecting rural life, the poor, the sick, the suffering, and the oppressed. From those stories, Jesus reminded his listeners to think of those with nowhere to go. In that 'not-so-direct way,' He left them themselves to reflect on their lives and the way of life of those in the upper echelons of society.

While only God knows all the reasons why Jesus used "stories" the way He did, we can only deduce within our limited minds perhaps a few: to hide truths from certain people and to enlighten further many of his listeners so that the leaders of His time will follow along with God's plans for them; to avoid alienating people from him and to reveal God's plans for them.

God, in His infinite love for us, revealed these teachings through Jesus. The richness of His teachings, filled with love and compassion, enabled us to better understand His mission to save the world and fulfill God's plans for all of us. *For God so loved the world that he gave his only Son so that everyone who believes in him might not perish but might have eternal life (John 3:16).* This profound love is a constant reminder of our worth and significance in His eyes.

Jesus did all these through his apostles, igniting the faith in what we and the world know now. Who could ever know that with only twelve whom He chose first, that unprecedented number could ignite a fire that multiplied a multitude of believers that can transform the faith and the world into what we now know? Their love of God through Jesus, the begotten Son of God, and through keeping his commandments and the resurrection conquered whatever fears remained in them. And as disciples and followers of Jesus Christ, that includes us. *For the love of God is this, that we keep his commandments. And his commandments are not burdensome, for whoever is begotten by God conquers the world. And the victory that conquers the world is our faith. Who [indeed] is the victor over the world but the one who believes that Jesus is the Son of God? (1 John 5:3-5)*

No one can ever fathom the extent of righteousness the parables of Jesus have done to the world as we see it today. No one can underestimate what we see in our world, the good those parables and "stories" have fulfilled or made possible.

CHAPTER 6

God's WORD

"My son, to my words be attentive, to my sayings incline to my ear; Let them not slip out of your sight, keep them within your heart; For they are life to those who find them, to man's whole being they are health. With closest custody, guard your heart, for in it are the sources of life."
– Proverbs 4:20-23

As Christians, we can attest to the profound transformation that stories about Jesus Christ have brought to our lives. These narratives, which have become integral to many, are not mere tales, but the living Word of God. Jesus, in his storytelling, touched on every aspect of human existence-life, hope, joy, love, struggles, and peace. His stories encompassed sickness and healing, hardness of heart and conversion, and even death. From these divine narratives, unique parables have emerged, inspiring and transforming the world.

Among the greatest stories ever told are those of Jesus Christ himself. His words and deeds, chronicled by the Prophets and the four holy Evangelists, St. Mark, St. Matthew, St. Luke, and St. John, are the epitome of storytelling. We have also heard or read about the saints and the Early Fathers of the Church, who have penned countless books and novels. They delved into the wisdom of past ages, affirming the Word of God and the prophets, and recounting the Lord's power to save and the wonders He had wrought. We honor the wisdom of their words. Through their writings, God beckons us to take heart, believe in their truths, and most importantly, to share. God calls us to proclaim His

word and share these stories, all for the glory of our Lord Jesus Christ—
God's WORD.

The treasury of the greatest stories ever told is vast and diverse, penned by the most significant authors and storytellers of the past and present. Each story is a unique testament to the power and grace of our Lord Jesus Christ, waiting to be discovered and shared.

Prayer: *Almighty Father, guard our hearts and minds, for in them are the sources of your Light. Help us always to be attentive to you. Never let us separate from you. May the word of Christ dwell among us in all its richness. Glory to you Word of God, Lord Jesus Christ. Amen.*

CHAPTER 7

Everything Begins And Ends With The WORD

"I am the Alpha and the Omega," says the Lord God, 'the one who is and who was and who is to come, the almighty.'"
– Revelation 1:8

"I am the Alpha and the Omega, the first and the last, the beginning and the end."
– Revelation 22:13

The WORD, or the Word of God, is used interchangeably to refer to Jesus Christ, the Son of God. *"And the Word became flesh and made his dwelling among us, and we saw his glory, the glory as of the Father's only Son, full of grace and truth."(John 1:14)*. This declaration in John's Gospel reminds us Who Jesus is, the Father's only Son, the Word incarnate, possessed of everything that is infinitely good and eternally true.

The declaration also unveils the awe-inspiring reason why St. John, the Evangelist, employed "The Word" at the commencement of his gospel. *"In the beginning was the Word, and the Word was*

The Child Jesus

with God, and the Word was God. He was in the beginning with God. All things came to be through him, and without him, nothing came to be." (John 1: 1-5). This segment of the prologue speaks of a pre-existence, one that the Christian tradition marvels at as Jesus Christ, the incarnate Word (in Greek, "Logos") that was instrumental in the creation of all things.[5] Without the Word, nothing came to be. (Ibid).

The Greek Word Logos means "word." To philosophers and theologians, it also implies thought, an expression of a truth or principle. The Bible Dictionary defines "word" as "a term of Latin origin signifying 'Word' used by St. John to designate the Son of God, for he is the complete 'expression' of the Father." (cf 1 Jn 1). In certain Greek philosophies, a mediator between God and creatures was called a Word. St. John also wanted to suggest that Christ, the Word of God, is the perfect mediator of creation and the divine life. (Rv 19, 11-16)."[6]

"Word" as defined, therefore, may also be used in the same manner as the Old Covenant and the New Testament may have given a more definite meaning to it, that Jesus is the revelation and communication of God to all of humanity and the world. God the Almighty Father revealed Himself through the prophets and the law in the Old Covenant. In the New Testament, God revealed Himself in the Person of Jesus Christ. In another part of the Scriptures, the Evangelist Matthew wrote that Jesus came to fulfill the law in "Do not think that I have come to abolish the law or the prophets. I have come not to abolish but to fulfill. (cf Matthew 5:17).

Prayer: Lord Jesus, may your words dwell among us in all their richness. Word of God, Son of the Father, Perfect Mediator of Creation and Divine Life, You who sit are the right of the Father to intercede for us, have mercy on us. Forgive us our sins and bring us to everlasting life. Glory to you Word of God, Lord Jesus Christ. Amen.

CHAPTER 8

The Sacred Scriptures Contain The Word Of God

"All scripture is inspired by God and is useful for teaching, for refutation, for correction, and for training in righteousness, so that one who belongs to God may be competent, equipped for every good work."
– 2 Timothy 3:16-17

In the Dogmatic Constitution on Divine Revelation *(Dei Verbum)*, we find in 6.24 that *[...] the Sacred Scriptures contain the word of God and since they are inspired really are the word of God; and so the study of the sacred page is, as it were, the soul of sacred theology.*

The Old Testament is reaffirmed by our Lord himself. The Sacred Scriptures contain the Word of God. The Catechism of the Catholic Church (CCC) wrote of this in CCC 129 and in CCC 135: *"As an old saying put it, the New Testament lies hidden in the Old and the Old Testament is unveiled in the New.[7] The Sacred Scriptures contain the Word of God and, because they are inspired they are truly the Word of God."[8]*

Many other passages point to Jesus as the perfect revelation of God Himself in the flesh or to Jesus as the Word of God:

In *John 14:9-10*, we are reminded of these words: *"Jesus said to him 'Have I been with you so long a time and you still do not know me, Philip? Whoever has seen me has seen the Father. How can you say, Show us the Father? Do you not believe that I am in the Father and the Father is in*

THE WORD IS WITH US

me? The words that I speak to you I do not speak on my own. The Father who dwells in me is doing his works."

In the following verses, Jesus speaks of sublime supplications to the Father:

"I cannot do anything on my own; I judge as I hear, and my judgment is just, because I do not seek my own will but the will of the one who sent me."(John 5:30).

"Everything that the Father gives me will come to me, and I will not reject anyone who comes to me, because I came down from heaven not to do my own will, but the will of the one who sent me."(John 6:37-38).

In the 17th chapter of John's gospel, Jesus, in his divine wisdom, prayed to the Father: "Now they know that everything you gave me is from you because the words you gave to me I have given to them, and they accepted them and truly understood that I came from you, and they have believed that you sent me. (John 17:7-8). These spirit-filled words, penned by St. John, echo the unity of the sublime truth and understanding of the relationship we have with Jesus, the beloved Son of the Almighty Father.

1 Corinthians 8:6 is an expression of a relationship in a personal and Christian way about Jesus Christ: "Yet for us there is one God, the Father, from whom all things are and for who we exist, and one Lord, Jesus Christ, through whom all things are and through whom we exist." We are God's creation; therefore, we exist for God. Through Jesus Christ, the beloved Son of God, all things, including us, exist.

Jesus asked the Father in prayer to glorify him: "I glorified you on earth by accomplishing the work that you gave me to do. Now glorify me, Father, with you, with the glory that I had with you before the world began. (John 17:3-5).

God personified Himself through the written and spoken word – in God the Son. God made flesh. The Lamb of God who takes away the sin of the world. (cf John 1:29) And He dwells among us. (cf John 1:14). And He loves us unconditionally. He is in our hearts and in our minds. He is Emmanuel, God with us. He helps us navigate our journey through life here on earth. Bishop Oscar Cantu of the Diocese of San Jose, California writes, "Jesus is the Word who informs and molds our hearts and minds in Love, Truth, and Beauty; the bread of life and the Cup of Salvation nourish us on the long and sometimes arduous journey of life and faith."[9]

In Jesus, with Jesus, and through Jesus, everything begins and ends with Him.

Prayer: *Lord Jesus, You are the perfect revelation of the Father Himself in the flesh; Lord have mercy. Christ Jesus, You are the Son of God and Son of Mary, Christ have mercy. Lord Jesus, You are Mighty God and Prince of Peace, Lord have mercy. May Almighty God have mercy on us, forgive our sins, and bring us to everlasting life. Amen.*

CHAPTER 9

The Alpha And Omega
And The Chi-Rho

"I am the Alpha and the Omega, 'says the Lord God,' the one who is and who was and who is to come, the almighty."'
– Revelation 1:8

The phrase' alpha and Omega' holds significant importance in the context of the Book of Revelations. It is first mentioned in the very first chapter, and we also find a similar reference in the 44th chapter of Isaiah. The phrase is derived from the first and last letters of the classical Greek alphabet, and when formed into a phrase, it signifies that Jesus has existed for all eternity. This interpretation has led dictionaries and Bible commentators to attribute this exact title phrase to Christ and God.

The phrase *'I am the Alpha and the Omega'* is further clarified by the addition of the words' *the beginning'* and *'the end* ' in *Revelation 21:6*. Here, it is not just a statement of Jesus' eternal nature, but also a promise of life-giving water to the thirsty. This promise, filled with hope and anticipation, is a testament to the abundant life that Jesus offers.

The phrase' Alpha and Omega' is reiterated in *Revelation 22:13*, underscoring the concept of Jesus as *the Alpha and Omega.* The verse emphasizes His imminent arrival and the recompense He will bring to each according to their deeds. This repetition further solidifies the understanding of Jesus as the first and the last, the beginning and the end.

In the early days of Christianity, Alpha and Omega were not just letters, but significant Christian symbols. These symbols were often seen in Church art, sometimes combined with the Cross and Chi-rho. They represented the triumphant God who had conquered death and sin. The symbols also found their place in Church liturgy, depicted in the liturgical vestments worn by bishops, priests, and deacons, further emphasizing their importance in the Christian faith.

The symbols Alpha and Omega with the Chi-rho
shown here embroidered in a deacon stole

One of the most common symbols in Christian art is the Chi-Rho. As a symbol for "Christ," the Chi Rho is written by superimposing the two Greek letters "Chi (X)" and "Rho (P)," which are the first two letters in Greek of the name of "CHRist."[10] The symbol was, in ancient times, believed to be pre-Christian in origin. Still, it wasn't until Constantine the Great that the symbol became more significant.[11]

Prayer: *Almighty God and Father, from whom all things are and for whom we exist. Dear Lord, Jesus Christ, through whom all things are and through whom we live, and O Holy Spirit who enkindles in us the fire of God's Love, we praise You, give You thanks, and give You glory for giving us Life. Hear us, King of eternal glory. Blessed are You, the alpha and omega of our faith, for You called us out of darkness into your marvelous light. Give us strength in temptation, endurance in trial, and gratitude in prosperity. We love You above all things. Never permit us to be separated from You. Amen.*

CHAPTER 10

God Sent Us His WORD To Be With Us

"In their distress they cried to the LORD, who saved them in their peril, Sent forth the word to heal them, snatched them from the grave. Let them thank the LORD for such kindness, such wondrous deeds for mere mortals."
– Psalm 107:19-21

The Father has bestowed upon us His Word, Jesus Christ, a beacon of hope and healing. His Word is not just a guide, but a transformative force that can lift us from the perils of certain death. It is a lamp for our feet, illuminating our path so that we may not be lost. He, the Mighty One, wishes to teach us and lead us on the path He has laid down for us. Through Him, we will come to the fullness of joy in His presence. Let us reflect on the wisdom of the Psalmist in *Psalms 16: 5-8, 11*:

"LORD, my allotted portion and my cup, you have made my destiny secure. Pleasant places were measured out for me; fair to me indeed is my inheritance. I bless the LORD who counsels me; even at night my heart extols me. I keep the LORD always before me; with the LORD at my right, I shall never be shaken. ...You will show me the path to life, abounding joy in your presence, the delights at your right hand forever."

To truly experience the joy in His presence, we need to open not just our minds and souls, but our hearts as well. Our lips should be filled with confession and gratitude for His gifts and blessings. As St. Paul beautifully articulates in *Romans 10:8b-10*: "*But what does it say? 'The word is near you, in your mouth and in your heart' (that is, the word of faith which we preach). For if you confess with your mouth that Jesus is Lord, and believe in your heart that God raised him from the dead, you will be saved. For one believes with the heart and so is justified, and one confesses with the mouth and so is saved.'*" This is the path to God's kingdom, true joy and peace.

The Lord is not just a distant figure, but the living water and the fountain of grace. He is not a passive observer, but an active helper. The Lord is our strength, our companion who walks with us in our journey. He meets us where we are, in our moments of doubt and fear. We are reminded of Saint Paul's words, "*I have the strength for everything through him who empowers me.*"*(Philippians 4:13)*. These words are a testament to the Lord's unwavering support and strength.

When we feel weak and overwhelmed by our tasks and anxieties, we can find strength in St. Paul's words to the Corinthians: "*... but he said to me, 'My grace is sufficient for you, for power is made perfect in weakness.' I will rather boast most gladly of my weaknesses, in order that the power of Christ may dwell with me. Therefore, I am content with weaknesses, insults, hardships, persecutions, and constraints, for the sake of Christ; for when I am weak, then I am strong.*"*(2 Corinthians 12:9-10)*.

When we are fearful and lacking in strength to go on, these words from the Prophet Isaiah are a potent reminder:

He gives strength to the fainting; for the weak he makes vigor abound. Though young men faint and grow weary, and youths stagger and fall, They that hope in the LORD will renew their strength, they will soar as with eagle's wings; They will run and not grow weary, walk and not grow faint." *(Isaiah 40: 29-31)*. These words enjoins us that we must wait, for the Lord renew our strength.

This line from 1 Peter is a constant inspiration: "*As newborn babies, desire the sincere milk of the word, that you may grow thereby.*" *(1 Peter 2:2)* As His children, our growth in the Spirit from our baptism depends on that precious milk of salvation, so that when the time comes, we may come to join Him in heaven.

This exhortation from the writer of Acts gives so much encouragement for us to grow more in faith: "*And now, I commend you to God, and to that gracious word of his that can build you up and give you the inheritance among all who are consecrated." (Acts 20:32).* The Word enables us with the help of His grace to grow and someday receive the inheritance promised by God.

In times of trouble, the Psalmist's words that follow gives us so much hope when we are in distress: *"Then call on me in times of distress; I will rescue you, and you shall honor me." (Psalm 50:15).*

The Lord hears us when we cry for help: *"The LORD has eyes for the just and ears for their cry. The LORD's face is against evildoers to wipe out their memory from the earth. When the just cry out, the LORD hears and rescues them from all distress. The LORD is close to the broken-hearted, saves those whose spirit is crushed." (Psalms 34:17-19).*

During my Morning or Evening Prayers, I often find a word or phrase from the Liturgy of the Hours or from the Christian Prayer Book that resonates with me. These moments of connection are precious, and I make sure to jot down these insights at the end of my prayers. I always keep a pen and a writing pad nearby for this purpose.

These moments of connection with God's Word are transformative. Some of the writings in this book are the fruits of these *graced* moments. Indeed, words of wisdom come to us mysteriously- words of beauty and love, words of hope and inspiration. These words have the power to stay with us, if we allow them to, and they inspire us to offer a prayer of thanksgiving to the Lord.

Prayer: *Good and loving God, we thank You for the words of wisdom that You, in your love for us, have allowed to come to us: words of beauty and love, words of hope and inspiration, words that You allow to stay and remain in our memory. We thank You for sending your Word, Jesus Christ, to us. Let your Word guide our paths always. May the word of Christ dwell among us in all its richness. Enable us to do all things through Him who strengthens us. Glory to you Word of God, Lord Jesus Christ. Amen.*

PART TWO

GOD IS ALWAYS WITH YOU

*"I keep the LORD always before me; with the LORD
at my right, I shall never be shaken."*
– Psalm 16:8

...."And behold, I am with you always, until the end of the world."
– Matthew28:20

God is always with you. Do you ever wonder why, even in our church liturgy and prayers, we say, "The Lord is with you"? In our tradition, that phrase, in all its meaning and wonder, is central to our faith. The Lord is with you because the Lord is your guardian and protector. Psalm 121:8 even attests to this: *"The Lord will guard your coming and going both now and forever."*

Even in the depths of your distress, when fear threatens to overwhelm you, God is always with you. Remember these words from Psalm 23:4: *"Even when I walk through a dark valley, I fear no harm for you are at my side; your rod and staff give me courage."* These words are beacons of hope, a reminder that God is always with you, even in the darkest times.

When you as a human being reach a point where there seems to be no more hope, Matthew 19:26 reminds you and me, *"...for human beings this is impossible, but for God all things are possible."*

God is always with you. The prophet Isaiah has these words: whenever fear engulfs you, and you need a firm helping hand, the Lord is always with you to help you. *"For I am the Lord your God, who grasps your right hand; It is I who say to you, 'Fear not, I will help you.' Fear not O worm, Jacob, O maggot Israel; I will help you, says the LORD; your redeemer is the Holy One of Israel. I will make of you a threshing sledge, sharp, new, and double-edged, To thresh the mountains and crush them, to make the hills like chaff." – Isaiah 41:13-15.*

People know when God is with them. For example, they might mysteriously encounter a stranger or a friend, leading them to believe that the encounter occurred because of God's providence. Some might also think it was just a coincidence. What was that? Others experience the divine in various ways or forms, such as miraculous healing, a life-changing incident, or an overwhelming feeling of peace.

Others may experience God's presence through a song or Scripture. Others may not hear or see anything but know that the Holy Spirit has just visited them deep in their hearts or minds.

Still, others may experience feelings of joy, love, beauty, and peace beyond words to express. They also know this happens only in God's grace and the workings of the Holy Spirit.

God's presence is not a fleeting moment but a constant assurance. He promises that He will never leave you or forsake you, *as Matthew 28:20* reminds us. In Hebrews 13.5, we also find these words: " ... *I will never forsake you or abandon you. The Lord is my helper,[and]I will not be afraid. What can anyone do to me?"* These words are a rock-solid foundation for your faith, a reminder that God's presence is unwavering, and it can strengthen your trust in Him.

Prayer: *Almighty God, Lord Jesus, Holy Spirit, you promised us that You will never forsake us or leave us. Keep us always in your sight. We praise, bless, adore, and glorify you for your great glory. Amen.*

CHAPTER 1

God Is With Us

*(Isaiah 7:10-14/ Romans 1:1-7/ **Matthew 1:18-24**)*
(GP: Luke 2:1-7)

Gospel: *Now, this is how the birth of Jesus Christ came about. When his mother Mary was betrothed to Joseph, but before they lived together, she was found with child through the holy Spirit. Joseph, her husband, since he was a righteous man, yet unwilling to expose her to shame, decided to divorce her quietly. Such was his intention when, behold, the angel of the Lord appeared to him in a dream and said, "Joseph, son of David, do not be afraid to take Mary your wife into your home. For it is through the holy Spirit that this child has been conceived in her. She will bear a son and you are to name him Jesus, because he will save his people from their sins." All this took place to fulfill what the Lord had said through the prophet: "Behold, the virgin shall be with child and bear a son, and they shall name him Emmanuel," which means, "God is with us." When Joseph awoke, he did as the angel of the Lord had commanded him and took his wife into his home. (Matthew 1:18-24)*

A few years ago, my wife and I embarked on an ocean cruise that traversed the majestic Suez Canal. This spiritual journey led us to Haifa, Tel Aviv, Athens, Croatia, Salalah, Oman, Dubai, Saudi Arabia, and various parts of the United Arab Emirates. We spent more days at sea than on land, aboard a colossal cruise ship teeming with over 3,000 passengers. This divine opportunity allowed us to marvel at the vastness of God's power and the beauty of His creation. There were days when we were greeted by nothing but the serene expanse of the ocean, until one fateful day when the monotony was shattered by an unexpected event-an event that would test our courage and resilience.

One day, as we were sailing toward Egypt, the ship's captain announced that two suspiciously-looking smaller vessels were approaching our boat. The ship captain said, there is a possibility that these could be pirates, you know, bad guys. So, we must take precautions. The first time I heard that, fear gripped me. I thought of the other passengers, hundreds of them, perhaps feeling the same way. But the curious character in me at that moment, Lita and I peeped through one of the windows inside where we were at that moment. As we happened to be near the aft, I saw two boats on the horizon. In that moment, I realized that fear was not the answer, but rather, it was our curiosity and resilience that would see us through. Thankfully, the situation was resolved without any harm, and we continued our journey with a newfound appreciation for the safety and security of our cruise ship.

A few moments later, the captain emphasized that all passengers must participate in a Safe Haven Drill. This is a crucial procedure for everyone's safety. All passengers on the outside decks are to proceed immediately to their rooms. It is of utmost importance that all passengers and non-essential crew members remain in their rooms until further notice. Those unable to return to their rooms immediately may proceed to the interior hallways inside the ship or to the theater, which are designated as safer areas.

"Do not be afraid. In times like this, we are required to conduct a Safe-Haven Drill. We just want to be prepared," the captain said through the PA system.

There are two things I would like to note here:

1. The words in this Gospel, where the angel of the Lord said, "… *do not be afraid".(cf Matthew 1:20)*
2. The ship's captain's words, "We just want to be prepared."

Even the most upright among us may find ourselves grappling with the fear of the uncertain. Yet, in the midst of this fear, we can find solace in our faith. Just as the word FEAR can be seen as an acronym for False Evidence Appearing Real, we can remember that our faith is a powerful tool in dispelling these false fears, offering us comfort and reassurance.

In the Gospel story, Joseph was a righteous man. Yet he feared people would discover Mary was with a child even before they lived together. This fear was not because he did wrong but because of what people might say, think, or do. Sometimes, we are even afraid that people might sense we are fearful of what is going on. We, too, try to cover up what we perceive to be wrong even if it is not faulty or hide what we think might cause embarrassment, which is not embarrassing after all. In other words, in many cases, we act only to please men, to avoid human judgment, which can be wrong. Joseph's story teaches us that even the most righteous can struggle with fear and the need for human approval, and it reminds us to trust in God's plan and not be swayed by human judgment.

Well, we see in the Gospel story how God intervenes as he did by sending an angel to tell Joseph not to be afraid. Let us be afraid of

God's judgment, not men. God's judgment is not about punishment or condemnation, but about His loving guidance and correction. It is about aligning our lives with His will and living in His love and grace. This brings us to my second point.

"We just want to be prepared."

The ship captain's precautions were to protect us from enemies *outside* who could harm and destroy us. But not all our enemies are outside us. Some are *within us,* and they are called *sins.* These 'enemies within us' are our negative thoughts, emotions, and actions that separate us from God's love and grace. From these and many other occasions of sin, Jesus comes to save us if we ask for help.

What are sins anyway? They are not just the breaking of rules. They are the manifestations of our worst instincts: anger, greed, lust, selfishness, irresponsibility, even cruelty. These are our 'enemies within us.' sometimes, we don't even need to act them out. We all know that there are times when we have these enemies within us. When we let them out, we harm others and ourselves. They keep us from reaching out to those who love or need us. They prevent us from doing good. They are destructive to our souls. These 'enemies within us' are the barriers that prevent us from fully embracing God's love and living according to His will.

Nothing can prepare us more than knowing that God is with us. 'Being with God' is not just about physical proximity or religious rituals, but about a deep and personal relationship with Him. It is about living in His presence, seeking His guidance, and trusting in His love and grace. After all, that is why Jesus is called *Emmanuel, 'God with us.'*

Like Joseph, a man of faith and prayer always has God on his side. Are we a people of faith and prayer? Do we strive to be like Joseph, a humble man who listens? Do we try to respond to the will of God? Joseph's story is a powerful example of faith, humility, and obedience. We must pray that we learn from St. Joseph's example and strive to emulate his virtues in our own lives.

Being with God is preparation. Being aware or at least knowing what we fear is preparation. These final hours of Advent offer us an opportunity to prepare and make ourselves fully ready for God to enter our world. Preparation, in this context, means aligning our hearts and minds with God's will, understanding our fears and weaknesses, and seeking God's guidance and strength to overcome them. It asks us to do what St. Joseph did: to prepare ourselves for God's will for our lives.

So, let us ask ourselves: what are the enemies within us, and how can we deal with them? When asking these questions, let us not be afraid. Prepare. Find time for quiet reflection. Find time to separate yourself from the season's stress and try to embrace your fears. Trust in the love of God. Go to confession.

When the captain of our cruise ship announced that we were returning to normal, it was a moment of relief for everyone. In that moment, I realized that the captain had not only brought us physical safety, but had also brought out the best in us. By embracing our fears, we had summoned more courage than usual, and had become more attentive to our responsibilities. This experience taught me the transformative power of courage and the relief it can bring.

Sometimes, we lean on our fears too much. Soon, we may find that our fears are unfounded. Or, sometimes, we find that they were just false appearances that seemed genuine.

Within ourselves, we can find relief from being attuned to the message that Jesus Christ is giving us. Preparation is the key. In a few days, we will celebrate the birth of our Lord and Savior, Jesus Christ. This is a joyful feast for many reasons. It is a time for family reunions, the exchanging of gifts, and acts of generosity to those in need. But most importantly, Christmas is a time to remember and celebrate the birth of Jesus Christ, who came to bring out the best in all of us and to save us from our sins. We must not be surprised about this because that's one of the many reasons why Jesus came – to bring out the best in all of us.

Prayer: *As we break bread together to celebrate the Holy Eucharist, let us thank God and ask for the grace to help us not to be afraid. To pray to Him to cast out all our fears, or to trust in Him when we lean too much on false uncertainties while the boat of our lives is in peril and to rely more on Him to bring out the best in all of us. May the word of Christ dwell among us in all its richness. Glory to you Word of God, Lord Jesus Christ. Amen.*

CHAPTER 2

We Are "Salt–Shakers" And "Light Bulbs" In The Life Of Others

*(Isaiah 58:7-10 / 1 Corinthians 2:1-5 / **Matthew 5:13-16**)*

Gospel: *You are the salt of the earth. But if salt loses its taste, with what can it be seasoned? It is no longer good for anything but to be thrown out and trampled underfoot. You are the light of the world. A city set on a mountain cannot be hidden. Nor do they light a lamp and then put it under a bushel basket.; it is set on a lampstand, where it gives light to all in the house. Just so, your light must shine before others, that they may see your good deeds and glorify your heavenly Father. (Matthew 5:13-16)*

Consider this: the Bible suggests that each of us, as Christians, is like a 'saltshaker' and a 'light bulb'. These metaphors, while not explicitly stated, are a unique way to describe our role. The Bible refers to Christians as the 'salt of the earth' and the 'light of the world' (*cf Matthew 5:13, 14*). But what does this really mean? How can we embody these metaphors in our daily lives, and what impact can they have on us and those around us?

In the context of ancient times, salt held immense value. It was even used as a gift to God, symbolizing the importance of offering something beneficial to humans as a way of honoring God. Salt was a commodity, a part of the rituals of sacrifices and burnt offerings.

"Hundreds of years ago, when babies were baptized, priests put a very tiny dub of salt in the baby's mouth as a way of blessing the baby at baptism. In ancient Europe, it was the custom that you shouldn't hurt anyone with whom you had eaten salt. The salt symbolized friendship, so you couldn't be mean to each other. When the Bible says that Christians are the salt of the earth, it means we are valuable, useful, and necessary. We are an important part of life. It is up to us not to lose our "flavor" or good qualities."[12]

Have you ever pondered what it means to be the light of the world? Perhaps you've found yourself in a dark room, unfamiliar to you as a child? To little children, this can be a terrifying experience. I can relate, as I too was once afraid of the dark. Now, as adults, our fears may have shifted, but they still exist. We've become cautious, always on the lookout for potential dangers. The fear of bumping our head or leg into something that could cause serious harm is ever-present. Who among us hasn't experienced an accidental trip while walking in an unlighted room that resulted in a mild or even serious injury?

"When you turn on the light, you can find your way around safely. Like a light, it is our responsibility to light up the world. We must make other people feel good and safe, and we must show people the way to God."[13]

My dear friends, as we delve into the readings today, let us remember that these are not just ancient texts, but living words that resonate with our daily lives. The 1st Reading from the Prophet Isaiah, for instance, speaks of ways of mercy to the stranger and neighbor, guiding us on how to reach out to those in the shadows of our society, a call that is relevant to each one of us.

Have you ever heard the phrase "like the dawn"? That phrase is an example that I would like to use to help us remember that we are not just passive observers, but active participants in the Gospel. Jesus calls his disciples the "light of the world," and that includes each one of us. We are not just witnesses to a new day, the onset of a new dawn, but we can provide a fresh, new outlook for the world as disciples of Jesus Christ. Our actions, as small as they may seem, can have a significant impact and make a difference in the lives of others. We must become living examples of God's love.

The 2nd Reading tells us what attitude we must have in doing such acts: a pure openness that trusts in God's power to act through us. St. Paul tells us how he came up with God's message for us. In humility, he writes with persuasive words in 1 Corinthians 2:5, "...*so that our faith might not rest on human wisdom but on the power of God.*"

How do we become a "light bulb" that could help light our path or that of others?

We become light by considering how people see us live in Christ. They see us as a "light bulb" that could serve as their light and guide. So that that "light bulb" would be of use and purpose to them, we are to ensure that we can provide the energy to keep it lit: no energy, no power, no light. We must preserve that energy so that it will be there when needed. In protecting that energy, enabling the "light bulb" to stay lit, we can be the light in the life of others.

We use up that energy if we use it only for ourselves. We can provide that light by not focusing on ourselves, not on our accomplishments that serve nobody except ourselves. We can be the source of that light by demonstrating the Spirit of God that accompanies and enlightens us in our relationships with others.

God reminds us to extend a genuine concern for the needy. One example is by doing justice to the needs of people experiencing poverty. Simply and actively, just "doing." We learn by doing, one of my Jesuit teachers always says. Experience is the best teacher. To experience what needs to be understood is the best way to practice what we teach.

Nothing can be accomplished without doing what needs to be done. After everything is said and expressed until one is "blue," just doing it is the key. Let this reminder inspire and motivate us to continue practicing acts of mercy and justice in our daily lives.

This brings us to remember the corporal acts of mercy. There are seven. Remember? They are *Feeding* the hungry, *giving drink* to the thirsty, *sheltering* the homeless, *visiting* the sick, *visiting* the incarcerated, *burying* the dead, and *giving* alms to the poor. Remember the active verbs. We learn by doing.

My dear friends, *doing* one of these acts of mercy for now would be a good start. With God's blessing, we can be the "salt of the earth" and the "light of the world." God is with us to help us *continue* and make that happen. With God, who is always with us, we can serve as the "light bulb" in the lives of others in Christ.

Prayer: *As we continue with our celebration of the Holy Eucharist, let us thank the Lord and ask for the grace to use us, to help us be able to taste and to see His grace in us, and through the power of that grace, to see ourselves as salt and light, for others and for the world. Lord, be our light to guide us always. Amen.*

CHAPTER 3

The WORD Is With Us

(Matthew 10:26-33)
(GP: Mark 4:22; 8:36; Luke 12:2-9; 8:17; 9:26)

Gospel: *Therefore, do not be afraid of them. Nothing is concealed that will not be revealed, nor secret that will not be known. What I say to you in the darkness, speak in the light; what you hear whispered, proclaim on the housetops. And do not be afraid of those who kill the body but cannot kill the soul; rather, be afraid of the one who can destroy both soul and body in Gehenna. Are not two sparrows sold for a small coin? Yet not one of them falls to the ground without your Father's knowledge. Even all the hairs of your head are counted. So do not be afraid; you are worth more than many sparrows. Everyone who acknowledges me before others I will acknowledge before my heavenly Father. But whoever denies me before others, I will deny before my heavenly Father. (Matthew 10:26-33)*

Fear no one! Three times, Jesus told his disciples not to fear. Jesus knew that fear was the most crippling of all emotions. When such emotions get you, there is no telling whether you can shake them off. Here is what Rev. Jess Esplana wrote about being afraid:

> "When I was a child, I was afraid of the dark. When I was a young man, I was afraid to speak in public,

because I was afraid to make mistakes. I was so tense during my first employment interview because I was afraid of not getting the job. I was scared waiting for the doctor's diagnosis and afraid to undergo surgery. I was scared of dying. I have no phobia, but the first time I rode a plane I developed cold feet. [...] there is always something of which we are afraid. This is normal. Even great men become afraid in given circumstances."[14]

This is fear in general. I have experienced the concerns in all of the above. For as long as we live, we experience the fear of the known and the unknown. But in our readings today, the question is not so much fear in general but the particular fear that Christians usually have when they must witness faith in God. It is the fear we experience the moment we witness that mysterious kingdom of justice, love, and compassion. The usual temptation is to keep silent. Because if not, we might rock the steady boat of friendly conversation. But must we?

In the Book of Acts, we encounter a powerful example of overcoming fear. St. Paul, when he arrived in Corinth, initially hesitated to preach there. However, he was not deterred by his fear. Instead, he found the strength to continue when the Lord appeared to him in a vision, reassuring him of his purpose: *"...Do not be afraid. Go on speaking, and do not be silent, for I am with you. No one will attack or harm you..." (Acts 18:9-10a)*. Every time I speak, preach, or venture into unfamiliar places, this scripture passage resonates with me. It's not just a set of words, but a personal guide that I turn to. Praying and seeking God's help before any endeavor has become a non-negotiable for me. This passage has been a steadfast companion throughout my journey, a reminder that the Word is always with us, and that God's transformative presence is ever-present in the world.

When the Lord commissioned his disciples to spread the Gospel, care for the poor, heal the sick, and cast out demons, he was well aware of the challenges they would face. He knew they would encounter opposition, and yet, he sent them forth, trusting in their faith and resilience.

The relevance of the 1st Reading in our lives today is evident in the story of Jeremiah. Despite his fear, he found the strength to pray and reassure himself. Reflecting on the words of this prophet, we can draw inspiration and guidance for our own journeys, *"The Lord is with me, like a mighty champion: my persecutors will stumble, they will not triumph." (Isaiah 20:11).* Jeremiah is an expert in honest and simple prayer. We should all learn from him!

One of my favorite psalms is the one our choir sang for us today. We joyfully sang with them, too. We sang beautifully and prayerfully to our heart's content. With confidence, we all sang, *"To you, O Lord, I lift up my soul. Lift up my spirit to my God. ...guide me...(cf Psalm 25:1, 5).*

The fear of the uncertain, some people say, reveals a lack of self-confidence. Maybe. Still, others say that fear comes from lacking faith or not having enough faith. Perhaps. God alone has the power to control life and death. Faith is like a shield of armor because it protects. Faith makes one courageous and unafraid. We feel good when our loved ones assure us that if we have faith, we will be alright, safe, and secure, and when they care. But who cares more than our heavenly Father?

Jesus cares for the poor and all of us because, in his eyes, we are more than the sparrows. Even the hairs on our heads are counted. If we are afraid, we need to pray like the apostles, *"...increase our faith." (Luke 17:5).* Lord, increase my faith.

My brothers and sisters, just call on the Lord. The Lord is just around waiting for us.

Last month, I asked Pastor Father Bob and our beloved Bishop Patrick to assign me to serve as a parish deacon at St. Catherine's in Morgan Hill, my old home parish. It was difficult for me to leave this parish and my diaconal ministries, particularly running the pantry, our outreach to feed the poor and the homeless, and helping organize the Bereavement Ministry here in our parish. I am proud of the work we have done together and the lives we have touched.

Most Holy Trinity (MHT) parish was my first assignment here in our Diocese of San Jose since my ordination on May 12, 2012, by our dear Bishop, Most Reverend Patrick Joseph McGrath. I must have done okay since Fr. Eddie recruited me because I am still here, looking healthy and alive, smiling before you. I am deeply grateful to God for the opportunity to serve and for the support and love I have received from this community. I am now at the end of my 5th year as one of your Permanent Deacons at MHT.

Each one of you, from the bottom of my heart, I want to express my deepest gratitude for your undying support and love. Our current Pastor, Fr. Bob, all our priests, deacons, and staff here at Most Holy Trinity, and Bishop Patrick, I am truly grateful for your guidance and friendship. But it is your love and friendship, which I will always hold dear, that has made my diaconal service here so memorable.

As I prepare to leave, I want to assure you that my prayers for you will continue. Today marks my last Sunday assisting and preaching at this Mass, and it is with a heavy heart that I bid my leave. But please know, I will not forget you. I humbly ask for your prayers as I embark on my new assignment as one of the permanent deacons at St. Catherine's Parish in Morgan Hill, a place that has been my home parish for 18 + years. Thank you, and may God bless you **all.**

Prayer: *As we continue celebrating the Holy Eucharist, let us thank God for the many blessings He has bestowed upon this parish and all of us; let us ask God for the grace to help us persevere and endure when fear and hardships come into our lives. Let us ask God to stay with us, give us the confidence that He is present in us, and know that His grace is sufficient for us. May the word of Christ dwell among us in all its richness. Let us also pray that we continue to be faithful in our dealings with people and generous with others, especially those in the shadows of our society; to cherish and enjoy the company of friends and loved ones; increase our love and strength of will for doing good not only for ourselves but also for others, for the greater glory of God and for the benefit of our souls. Glory to you Word of God, Lord Jesus Christ. Amen.*

CHAPTER 4

God Knows Who You Are

(Matthew 16:13-20)
(GP: Mark 8:27-30; Luke 9:18-21; John 6:67-71)

Gospel: *When Jesus went into the region of Caesaria Philippi he asked his disciples, "Who do people say that the Son of Man is?" They replied, "Some say John the Baptist, others Elijah, still others Jeremiah or one of the prophets." He said to them, "But who do you say that I am?" Simon Peter said reply, "You are the Messiah, the Son of the living God." Jesus said to him in reply, "Blessed are you, Simon son of Jonah. For flesh and blood has not revealed this to you, but my heavenly Father. And so, I say to you, you are Peter and upon this rock I will build my church and the gates of the netherworld shall not prevail against it. I will give you the keys to the kingdom of heaven. Whatever you bind on earth shall be bound in heaven; and whatever you loose on earth shall be loosed in heaven." Then he strictly ordered his disciples to tell no one that he was the Messiah. (Matthew 16:13-20)*

In my homilies, I often stress that the Gospels are *not just stories, but personal encounters* with Jesus. I hold this belief strongly. I also believe that in these encounters, God is speaking directly to us. I pose questions that aim to deepen, clarify, and inspire these encounters. How does this Gospel personally connect you with Jesus? How can we apply these encounters to our modern lives?

The essence of today's Gospel is not confined to the pages of scripture, but it unfolds in our daily lives. This is not a game of chance, but a reality that we experience here and now.

There are walls, like barriers, that obstruct our worship. There are hindrances, like roadblocks, that prevent us from encountering Jesus. The consequence of these obstacles is our potential inability to recognize the Messiah. Allow me to illustrate this with a few examples using this quote:

> "Maybe it's our work, our food, our toys, our image, our egos... it is all the things that we hold, near and dear. And Christ lovingly comes to each of us, with our weeds growing from within our wheats, while we carry the same faults and indiscretions found in Peter and his disciples. Jesus asks you and me, the same question – "Who do you say that I am?" [...] And Peter was the one who answered correctly and with authority. We are told that his answer was revealed to him by God. In short – it came from within."[15]

The long answer comes from St. Paul in the 2nd Reading. He wrote, *"For from him and through him and for him are all things."* Everything, without exception, originates from Him. The Lord and Giver of all life. The Alpha and the Omega. The first and the last. Contemplate the myriad of possibilities, and you will find no end. The sheer richness, immensity, and power of this, as penned by the Apostle to the Gentiles, is the genesis of all conceivable answers to the question.

In his letter to the Romans, Paul also wrote that God confirms who we are so that we may know him. Can you, too, fathom that God affirms that you can know yourself better if your heart and mind are open to His *grace?*

Through our baptisms, we are summoned to emulate Christ. By virtue of baptism, we become integral to Christ's prophecy and priesthood, perpetuating the faith. Let us never lose sight of the fact that we are a parish church and a community that loves as God loves.

Our mission statement at St. Catherine's is a call to action: '*We are called to live and proclaim the good news of Jesus Christ through worship, discipleship, and service.'* Like Peter in the Gospel, who was blessed with such a divine encounter, we too must be receptive to this grace. How? By actively turning away from our sins, from our false gods, and living out our mission as a parish church and a loving community.

The answer also resides within us. From within our families. From our relationships with our families and in the Church. When we love and forgive When we serve in various ways in our ministries and set out to reach out to people experiencing poverty and those in need.

We have many ministries here at St. Catherine, like Stephen Ministry, that can let us actively express the answer to the question in Christ's love. We reach out to those who face the many challenges in life and listen to them with an open mind. In many ways, as disciples, we not only worship and pray but come *"to serve and not to be served"* by listening and reaching out to them.

Prayer: *Almighty God and Father, we ask for your grace to enable us to give the gift of ourselves as best we can by serving and being an instrument of your Son, our Lord, our model of care and compassion. Help us so that through how we serve others, we make the face of Christ more visible to all people around us. May the word of Christ dwell among us in all its richness. Have mercy on our poor souls so that by prayerfully examining ourselves and with your grace, we can know who we are and who Christ is to us. Amen.*

CHAPTER 5

Where Is My Room?

(Exodus 24:3-8; Hebrews 9:11-15; **Mark 14:12-16, 22-26)**
(GP: Matthew 26:17-20, 26-29; Luke 22:7-20)

The Most Holy Body and Blood of Christ

Gospel: *On the first day of the Feast of Unleavened Bread, when they sacrificed the Passover lamb, his disciples said to him, "Where do you want us to go and prepare for you to eat the Passover?" He sent two of disciples and said to them, "Go into the city and a man will meet you, carrying a jar of water. Follow him. Wherever he enters, say to the master of the house, 'The teacher says, "Where is my guest room where I may eat the Passover with my disciples?"' Then he will show you a large upper room furnished and ready. Make the preparations for us there." The disciples then went off, entered the city, and found it just as he had told them; and they prepared the Passover.*

...While they were eating, he took bread, said the blessing, broke it, and gave it to them, and said, "Take it, this is my body." Then he took a cup, gave thanks, and gave it to them, and they all drank from it. He said to them, "This is my blood of the covenant, which will be shed for many. Amen, I say to you, I shall not drink again the fruit of the vine until the day when I drink it new in the kingdom of God." Then, after singing a hymn, they went out to the Mount of Olives. (Matthew 14:12-16, 22-26)

A few years ago, doctors believed a rare mosquito bit my older brother in the Philippines. He became so sick that he needed an immediate blood transfusion. He needed fresh, pure, and untainted blood compatible with his own. His son gave him that much-needed life-giving blood, which extended my brother's life for many months. Blood heals. Blood keeps us alive and well.

Some of you may have experienced giving or donating blood to save or extend the life of someone or someone who might need it someday. I have, and if you have done this, then you know the process and meaning of it all. It is one very profound experience. I had such an experience. And, in those moments lying on my back, as I watched the collection bag slowly filling, I could not help but think of how vital blood is to life and the sacredness with which it is regarded in every culture.

Doctors will also tell you that giving your blood creates or allows room or space for new cells to develop and produce in your blood system. Thanks to medical science, we know much about blood's complex, life-giving nature.

A few years ago, we heard on the news that scientists found that a single drop of blood would revolutionize how we fight blood diseases. With that one drop of blood, science can now tell us that every virus the body has—more than 200 viruses affects humans.

Here is what Michael Bulson wrote about blood

> "Even in our modern age, to our knowledge, no one has come with an artificial substitution for blood. Although ancient people did not have this knowledge, they had a deep respect for this mysterious liquid."[16]

It's truly remarkable. In the early Jewish and Hebrew traditions, blood was deeply intertwined with life. This concept is echoed in the readings, where 'blood' is mentioned nine times. However, in the Gospel, Jesus presents a new perspective on blood, viewing it as a sacrificial element. As the Lamb of God, Jesus elevates the concept of sacrifice to a new level. He establishes the Eucharist, a memorial of his sacrificial suffering and death, his body offered, and his blood outpoured, through which we are reconciled with God.

Understanding the significance of sacrifice, we recognize why the Eucharist, or the Holy Mass, is the focal point of our faith-the origin and pinnacle, the source and summit, of our beliefs. Through the Holy Mass, Christ invites us to participate in His sacrifice, to unite as a community of disciples, to commune, to worship, and to forever express our gratitude to Him as our Savior. Thus, we aspire to perceive these moments as profound encounters with Jesus Christ through our Holy Communion with Him.

The Gospel passage today serves as a reminder that we have 'prepared a room' for Jesus. This reminder is not solely directed at his disciples, but also at us. As we often encounter in various parts of the Scriptures, the Word of God speaks of divine encounters; here, Jesus is referring to an encounter with Him. What does Jesus mean by this metaphorical 'room '?

That "room" is our heart. We can listen to our heart. We can think with our hearts. We can act with our hearts. In prayer, we can ask God if what we do or wish to do is following his will. Know that the heart is the source of our life-giving flow of blood. The blood inside our bodies goes through the chambers of our hearts in every moment of our lives in a constant, continuous flow. If that flow stops, we can die. But Jesus stands at the door and knocks.

Are you prepared to extend that invitation? Through the acts of Confession and Holy Communion, we extend a personal invitation to Jesus to enter that room within us and make it His dwelling place. We humbly ask Jesus if it is His will to cleanse us. With His most precious blood, our sins are washed away, and our souls are transformed, pure as snow. This invitation is not a mere formality, but a deeply personal and significant act that makes us feel valued and included in His divine plan.

Prayer: *As we continue celebrating the Holy Eucharist to nourish our souls with the body and blood of Christ, let us thank the Lord and ask for Jesus to help us prepare the room for him, the room in our hearts. May the word of Christ dwell among us in all its richness. May the Word guide us and lead us. May the Lord never let us be separated from Him. Let us ask for God's grace so that we can prepare the room for Him in a way that pleases Him, where He can stay and live with us forever and ever. Amen.*

CHAPTER 6

Why Do You Go To Church?

*(Colossians 1: 24-2:3/ **Luke 6:6-11**)*

*Weekday Reflection while on a pilgrimage in
Lourdes, France September 11, 2017*

Gospel: *On another sabbath, he went into the synagogue and
taught, and there was a man there whose right hand was withered.
The scribes and the Pharisees watched him closely to see if he
would cure on the sabbath so that they might discover a reason to
accuse him. But he realized their intentions and said to the man
with the withered hand, "Come up and stand before us." And he
rose and stood there. Then Jesus said to them, "I ask you, is it
lawful to do good on the sabbath rather than to do evil, to save
life rather than to destroy it?" Looking around at them all, he then
said to him, "Stretch out your hand." He did so and his hand was
restored. But they became enraged and discussed together what
they might do to Jesus. (Luke 6:6-11)*

We have heard and seen specific stories in the Bible about the teachers
of the law and the Pharisees closely watching Jesus. They do this to find
something to accuse him of. I wrote this reflection while pilgrimaging
the Shrine of Our Lady in Lourdes, France, with Lita and a group of
parishioners. While preparing for this reflection, as you will see, I
thought the title should be why you go to church.

When we consider the reasons for attending church or places of worship, the first and foremost should be to worship and pray. This is the essence of our faith. Another crucial aspect is to give glory to God. A helpful guide in this regard is the pneumonic for **ACTS**— Adoration, Confession, Thanksgiving, and Supplication. These four elements encapsulate the essence of our worship. While there may be other reasons for this reflection, let us focus on ACTS and these core principles.

One of the most profound reasons for attending church is to express our gratitude to God. This act of thanksgiving is a powerful way to acknowledge the graces and blessings we have received. While there may be other reasons for this reflection, let us focus on this fundamental aspect of our faith.

Sometimes, you listen to some churchgoers, and sometimes, we wonder: Did they go to worship God? Because once the service is over, they come to you and share everything they found wrong while in the church. That is okay, too. But they see something they perceive as wrong with the priest's manner of doing the Mass or preaching the sermon. The sermon was too long. Or, he repeats and repeats himself. He said too much about sin. Oh yes, the deacon who preached, too! Oh, oh…

Mind you, deacons are also subject to this kind of criticism. Though, perhaps God has spared me as a receiver of these criticisms. In the event I will become the recipient of any criticism on my manner of serving at the Mass or preaching, I must take this kind of criticism in a positive light to the best of my God-given abilities. It compels me to practice this thing called "examination of conscience." The process can be "humbling." It can become educational. Sometimes, the result is some form of entertainment! Not only do you smile, but you also laugh! Not only do you think repeatedly, but you also go to your room and pray some more.

Here are a few more. People comment about latecomers as if they haven't been late to a Mass before their entire life. Fine. They criticize the "faithful departed" (those who leave before the Mass ends). Fine. They also complain about the crying and the noise caused by children, as if they didn't do such things when they were kids. Fine. They also express sadness about the absence of children or youth. Fine. But they

THE WORD IS WITH US

also complain about how people dress. Fine. And so on. Fine. The list goes on. Fine.

But wait, they also blame the parishioner or even the cook. Not fine. They question why they bring up financial needs while complaining why the walls on one side of the church outside are filthy. Oh yes, the parking space. There are too many cars now, and we need more parking space. Fine. I had to park and walk far. Not fine. Then, ask why the church has wobbly pews or insufficient air. And, of course, the choir! Fine and fine. Is there anything else?

Why do you go to church?

Prayer: *Father of Mercy and God of love, forgive our failings. Keep us in your peace and lead us in the way of salvation. Give us strength in serving You as followers of Jesus Christ. May the word of Christ dwell among us in all its richness. May You help us to remain faithful no matter what ails our surroundings. Teach us to be humble in the face of adversity. Amen.*

CHAPTER 7

God Stands By Us

*(Colossians 2: 6-15/ **Luke 6:12-19**)*
(GP: Matthew 10: 1-4; Mark 3:13-19a; John 1:42)

Feast of the Holy Name of the Blessed Virgin Mary
(Weekday Reflection while on a pilgrimage in
Fatima, Portugal, September 12, 2017)

Gospel: *In those days he departed to the mountain to pray, and he spent the night in prayer to God. When day came, he called his disciples to himself, and from there he chose Twelve, whom he named apostles: Simon, whom he named Peter, and his brother Andrew, James, John, Philip, Bartholomew, Matthew, Thomas, James the son of Alphaeus, Simon who was called a Zealot, and Judas the son of James, and Judas Iscariot, who became a traitor.*

And he came down with them and stood on a stretch of level ground. A great crowd of disciples and a large number of people from all Judea and Jerusalem and the coastal region of Tyre and Sidon came to hear him and to be healed of their diseases; and even those who were tormented by unclean spirits were cured. Everyone in the crowd sought to touch him because power came forth from him and healed them all. (Luke 6:12-19)

After my Morning Prayers, a sacred ritual in the Liturgy of the Hours, I often find myself in a state of serenity, perfect for jotting down brief reflections. The mind is completely tranquil in the stillness, especially before the sun's first light. These moments, for me, are the most opportune to commune with the Lord, as the mind has just emerged from a restful night.

This morning, in the peaceful town of Fatima, a quick glance from the hotel window reveals a serene scene. A few of the town's streetlights still illuminate the quiet streets. I can see only a handful of souls walking and cars gliding along the roads. I noticed a few women standing in front of an image of our Lady near the hotel, their silent prayers adding to the tranquility of the morning.

Remembering the Morning Prayer that my wife and I prayed together the day before reminded me to rest in the Lord more. Since it is Tuesday, today we can slow down.

How often do we experience this profound sense of resting in the Lord? Incredibly, countless times! This morning, however, is different. There was an immediate urge to pen this reflection, to set aside our plans for today's tour of Fatima and focus on the one itinerary that holds such immense importance. We are preparing to attend today's monumental outdoor Mass, followed by the evening procession, and Father and I will be there with our group.

A View of the grounds in front of the Church of Our Lady of Fatima, Portugal. Marian II Pilgrimage. September 2017

What came to mind was a line from the famous song *"Stand by Me".[17]* If you remember that song, it begins with: *"Stand by me. Oh, oh, stand by me."* That's why the title of this reflection is so significant. It's not just a philosophical idea, but a profound truth. God is not distant, *but stands by us,* ready to be embraced. When we open our hearts and minds to this truth, our faith becomes robust and transformative. Consider this: Our Christian faith is not built on philosophical ideas, but on a personal, life-changing relationship with God.

Our faith is unique. It is not a product of philosophical musings or religious doctrines. It is a result of a personal, exclusive relationship with one person – Jesus Christ. This relationship is the source of everything in our faith, making it a truly special and transformative journey.

In the very 1st Reading for today, Paul reminds us: *"So, as you receive Christ Jesus the Lord, walk in him, rooted in him and built upon him and established in the faith as you were taught, abounding in thanksgiving."* *(Colossians 2:6)* According to St. Paul, in Christ dwells the fullness of God. To Him, all cosmic power and authority belong. Christ connects the heavens and the earth.

St. Luke tells us in the Gospel today: *"Coming down the hill with them, Jesus stood on a level place."(cf Luke 6:17).* Jesus came down with his disciples. The Lord chose to stand with us. As disciples, we are one with God because He stands by us.

Leading the Candlelight Procession as a deacon, 100th Year Anniversary of the Our Lady of the Rosary of Fatima, in Ourem, Portugal, September 2017

Prayer: *May God give us grace, with the help of Our Lady of Fatima's prayers, to enable us to continue standing with Him, by Him, and gather around Him not only during this pilgrimage but always. May we always reach out to Him with our Mother's help. May we be blessed with the power that comes from Him to bring people to Him and to enable us to help the less fortunate and to hold them in our hearts. May we always be thankful that He stands by us. May the word of Christ dwell among us in all its richness. May the Word lead us and guide us. Glory to you Word of God, Lord Jesus Christ. Amen.*

PART THREE

WORDS OF WISDOM COME INTO OUR HEARTS

"For wisdom will enter your heart, knowledge will please your soul,
Discretion will watch over you, understanding will guard you."
– Proverbs 2:10-11

If we allow ourselves new hope, our lives can experience new beginnings. If we open ourselves to possibilities leading to a different view of circumstances happening in our midst, such a view might enable us to remove our fears. In doing so, we can prepare ourselves more readily. We can find what our heart is leading us to do. We can express what the Spirit of the Lord asks us to do. *"Either declare the tree good and its fruit is good or declare the tree rotten and its fruit is rotten, for a tree is known by its fruit....from the fullness of the heart the mouth speaks."* (Matthew 12:33-34).

It is a blessing for a man to speak his heart and lift his mind and thoughts in prayer to God. Unbeknownst to us, words of wisdom come into our hearts, our minds, then into our mouths, then into our tongues. *"Death and life are in the power of the tongue; those who make it a friend shall eat its fruit."* (Proverbs 18:21).

One of my favorite psalm-prayers that found its way to the Christian Prayer from the Liturgy of the Hours sounds like this: *"Make our mouths speak your wisdom Lord Jesus and help us to remember that you became man and redeemed us from death that we might merit the beauty of your light."[18]*

The words of the Prophet in *Jeremiah 1: 4-9* are the words the Lord places in our mouths. *"Then the Lord extended his hand and touched my mouth, saying, 'See, I placed words in your mouth.'"(Jeremiah 1:4–9).* How can those not be words of inspiration for us? Those are words of wisdom in our mouths for us to chew, taste, and express in all their beauty and splendor. In His grace, our Lord would desire for all of us to have them. We need to ask Him in prayer, and we shall receive. Or, if we haven't found the words to speak it, we must seek those words and pray that we may find it.

Prayer: *Almighty Father, help us to always remember your presence in us, especially in times of trouble. May the word of Christ dwell among us in all its richness. In prayer, we ask for your grace to speak your wisdom and express it in all its beauty and splendor. Glory to you Word of God, Lord Jesus Christ. Amen.*

CHAPTER 1

The Lord Sends Us
Words Of Wisdom

*"For the LORD gives wisdom, from his mouth come knowledge
and understanding; He has counsel in store for the upright,
he is the shield of those who walk honestly, Guarding the
paths of justice, protecting the way of his pious ones."*
– Proverbs 2:6-8

First, we hear them. Or we see them right before our eyes if we are
keenly watching. They might come while reading a book or listening to
the radio. Or live-streaming or watching a movie. Or while driving and
while we see people. They may come as a result of conversations with
people. Then, mysteriously, a desire to respond, whether it's a feeling of
awe, a need to share, or a curiosity to learn more, is triggered by what
we hear or see right before our eyes.

Sometimes, nothing happens at all. Where do those big words come
from? How does a word come to us or our minds? What comes to mind
are these words of the poetic homily, a form of religious discourse that
uses poetic language and imagery, from the Speaker in the Book of
Deuteronomy:

*"Give ear, O heavens, while I speak; let the earth hearken
to the words of my mouth! May my instruction soak in
like the rain, and my discourse permeate like the dew,*

like a downpour upon the grass, like a shower upon the
crops: For I will sing the Lord's renown. Oh, proclaim the
greatness of our God!" – Deuteronomy 32:1-3

The Lord sends us words of wisdom. If we have the ear for it, we can listen! Perhaps even the entire world can listen. The Almighty places the words in our mouths and if we allow Him with an open heart, we will hear His words. Of course, it happens because the Lord wants it to happen. Once it happens, He leaves us to our free will to do with it as we wish. God sees all that is. We have a choice. Perhaps this is why the Psalmist writes:

"Even before a word is on my tongue,
   LORD, you know it all.
Behind and before you encircle me.
   and rest your hand upon me.
Such knowledge is beyond me,
   far too lofty for me to reach. (Psalm 139:4-6)

After words are spoken, a spark of grace comes to our minds and hearts, recognizing the beauty of what we just thought and said out loud. Then something snaps into the mind, taking those words and committing them to memory—amazing grace. This recognition, this moment of inspiration, fills us with joy and satisfaction, and we are grateful for it.

We know it does happen when the Blessed Lord makes us realize it here and there. But sometimes, unbeknownst to us, it just happens. In mysterious ways, all of a sudden, we discover an excellent line for a poem there. Or, a burst of a short but surprisingly beautiful anecdote or story here. Or, there is a sudden spark of an idea and a word of inspiration here. Lots of gifts and blessings. Until we are blissfully satisfied and grateful to the Lord that in the likes of these words from the Prophet Jeremiah, such as, *"When I found your words, I devoured them; they became my joy and the happiness of my heart, Because I bore your name, O LORD, God of hosts." – (Jeremiah 15:16),* we can express them in gratitude.

Gifts from the Holy Spirit are what they all are. It is then up to us to find the time to capture those *sparks* in our hearts again and use them to benefit ourselves and others. Or the least we can do is to express them in ways that are pleasing in the sight of God to others. In time, we will know that, by grace, we will come to realize the beauty of it all. We can sing with a heart full of gratitude and love, just like what the Psalmist wrote in this love song:

> *My heart is stilled by a noble theme,*
> *as I sing my ode to the king.*
> *My tongue is the pen of a nimble scribe. (Psalm 45:2)*

Prayer: *Almighty God, Father of our Lord Jesus Christ, faith in your word is the way to wisdom, and to ponder your divine plan is to grow in the truth. May the word of Christ dwell among us in all its richness. Open our eyes, minds, hearts, souls to your deeds, ears to the sound of your call, and mouths so that every act may increase our sharing in the life You have offered us. Glory to you Word of God, Lord Jesus Christ. Amen.*

CHAPTER 2

An Echo From The Flock

"For thus says the Lord GOD: I myself will look after and tend my sheep. As a shepherd tend his flock when he finds himself among his scattered sheep, so will I tend my sheep. I will rescue them from every place where they were scattered when it was cloudy and dark."
– Ezekiel 34:11-12

Just like a sheep can easily get confused even in its environment, wander off, and be in harm's way without a shepherd, I, too, found myself in similar situations. But with the caller's voice and the flock's leader, the sheep will know where to go. The Shepherd gathers the flock, guiding them to safety and protection. This analogy holds a profound meaning in my personal narrative, reflecting the role of guidance and protection in my life.

Allow me to share a story that resonated deeply with me, inspired by the Gospel of Saint Mark. During my time in deacon formation, I was tasked with finding an excellent topic for an essay in my Catechesis class. It was then that this memory from my childhood, a memory that mirrored the teachings of the Gospel, came rushing back to me. Without a moment's hesitation, I knew I had found my topic.

I grew up in a farming community where farmers lead their carabaos and farm animals to pasture. My dad had a young carabao, which he received as payment for using a parcel of agricultural land the family owned. Like a shepherd, I took on the responsibility of riding and leading that baby carabao as part of its training in the rice fields. Before the end of the day, with my cousins, we gather all the beasts of burden and bring them home. I was usually late coming to the catechism class because of that. My aunts reported me to my dad for being late, so my dad did not want me to go out to do the pasturing anymore with my cousins if I did not watch my time. But because of the stubborn sheep in me, I still sneak out sometimes without his knowledge.

I was introduced to the catechism in English and the local vernacular.[19] I could not imagine where I am today in my faith journey had it not been for my spiritual shepherds. The people who taught me basic catechism growing up in the Philippines were my aunts and, of course, my parents, as well as a few other elderly folks. They "echoed"[20] what their fathers and mothers taught them and their parents before them: the WORD of God. "This 'echo' of the Word of God is catechesis."[21]

> "...the name catechesis was given to the whole of the efforts within the Church to make disciples, to help people believe that Jesus is the Son of God, so that believing they might have life in his name, and to educate and instruct them in this life and thus build up the Body of Christ."[22]

Our parents were catechists in their own right. They shared the fire enkindled by the Holy Spirit in their hearts with me, my siblings, and the community. I believe they were like the people described by Anne Marie Mongoven as "the strong, faithful people committed to sharing their faith, who have generously given of themselves for decades."[23]

Perhaps our parents also personified the apostles Peter and John, who taught in the name of Jesus Christ and boldly proclaimed it was impossible for them not to speak about what they have seen and heard (cf. Acts 4: 20). They promoted knowledge of the faith. However, they needed to be more keenly aware that, in so doing, they were fulfilling that first task of catechesis.[24]

Reflecting on my own journey, I recall the shepherds who taught me to pray and participate in liturgical life. My parents and aunts, in their God-given role, were the primary shepherds. Through their catechizing, they planted a sense of belonging to the community of disciples. They embarked on a missionary initiation, sharing their faith in its simplest forms and teachings. In their unique way, rooted in our culture, my parents and aunts were my first and foremost *agents* of catechesis as I grew up, a diversity I now appreciate.

As catechesis focuses on nurturing initial faith, it is the parents who hold the most influential role. They are the primary agents of catechesis, empowered to guide their children's spiritual journey.[25] Parents, as the first educators or catechists, hold a unique and irreplaceable role in our community. They bear the responsibility of teaching the Good News, a task that no one else can fulfill. As children of the Triune God, we all share in this mission through our baptism in Christ as priest, prophet, and king, in the anointing of the Holy Spirit, and in our participation in the Sacraments. We are all agents of catechesis, but parents, you are the pioneers.

When we catechize, we do so with the understanding that the Church's primary purpose is to evangelize. This is not just a task for the clergy or religious educators, but for all of us. Our understanding of catechesis, with Jesus Christ as its cornerstone and central focus, is what the Church builds upon and passes on to everyone. "As members of the Body of Christ, we are drawn to God's will, participating and uniting with Christ in his salvific work. We are his Church, and for Catholics, 'the Church exists to evangelize.'"(Pope Paul VI, *On Evangelization in the Modern World*, 14).[26]

What is the relationship between catechesis, revelation, and evangelization? At the heart of catechesis is "the Person of Jesus of Nazareth, 'the way, the truth and the life', and Christian living which consists in following the same Jesus to be in communion and intimacy with Him."[27] "In His goodness and wisdom, God chose to reveal Himself in Jesus, the incarnate Word, and to tell us the hidden purpose of the Father's will. Revelation is the act by which God communicates Self."[28]

Through this revelation, the invisible God, because of His abundant love, speaks to men as friends and lives among them.[29] Catechesis, as an ecclesial ministry, assists in making clear the core objectives of building initial faith, belief in Jesus Christ, calling individuals and community to a conversion, a transformation in life, a change of heart, and a renewed

Christian life. When God calls a change, transformation and renewal in the world happens.

A way to manifest or reach such change or renewal is, by the grace of God, catechesis and evangelization. It is in situating catechesis within the context of evangelization that the core objectives of catechesis are made clear.[30] In his mercy and love, God gave his only Son so that everyone who believes in him might not perish but might have eternal life. (cf. John 3:16)

In catechesis and evangelization, it is a proclamation in many and varied ways of the unconditional love of the Word of God, the One who is love, who pours that love out on humankind through Christ and the Holy Spirit. As members of His flock, our response would be to repeatedly return that same true love from us, creating an "echo" of His grace and love from the flock.

Prayer: *Lord Jesus, our Shepherd, your love for us is such that You will not leave us unattended, but your loving eyes are only focused on us. May your word dwell among us in all its richness. Help us to be able to maintain our gaze on You so that we may not go astray and fall into the valley of death. Help us always listen to your voice, the only one that could lead us to eternal life. Let us worship the Lord, for we are his people, the flock he shepherds, alleluia!*

CHAPTER 3

The Beginning Of An Incredible Journey

(Matthew 3:1-12)
(GP: Mark 1:2-8; Luke 3:1-18, John 1:19-28)

Gospel: *In those days, John the Baptist appeared, preaching in the desert of Judea [and] saying, "Repent, for the kingdom of heaven is at hand! It was of him that the prophet Isaiah had spoken when he said: "A voice of one crying out in the desert, 'Prepare the way of the Lord, make straight his paths.'" John wore clothing made of camel's hair and had a leather belt around his waist. His food was locusts and wild honey. At that time Jerusalem, all Judea, and the whole region around the Jordan were going out to him and were being baptized by him in the Jordan River as they acknowledged their sins.*

When he saw many of the Pharisees and Sadducess coming to his baptism, he said to them, "You brood of vipers! Who warned you to flee from the coming wrath? Produce good fruit as evidence of your repentance. And do not presume to say to yourselves, 'We have Abraham as our father.' For I tell you, God can raise up children to Abraham from these stones. Even now the ax lies at the root of the tree. Therefore every tree that does not bear good fruit will be cut down and thrown into the fire. I am baptizing you with water, for repentance, but the one who is coming after me is mightier than I. I am not worthy to carry his sandals. He will baptize with the holy Spirit and fire. His winnowing fan is in his hand. He will clear his threshing floor and gather his wheat into his barn, but the chaff he will burn with unquenchable fire." (Matthew 3:1-12)

After Thanksgiving Day, many people experience "turkey" fatigue. I am one of them. Many of us say, "Oh my goodness, now I have to think of Christmas!" I have a list of "to-do" things. Even preparing a list can often lead to anxiety, a feeling we all experience throughout the year. We become impatient. But God is patient with us, understanding that we are all on a journey and that change takes time. God is allowing us to recognize his patience with us. God waits. That is a gift, like Advent, a season that invites us to reflect, prepare, and find peace amidst our anxieties.

Advent is a gift – a time of waiting and preparing to welcome God as the Child. It is a time of openness to change, a willingness to let go of old habits and attitudes that hinder our relationship with God, and a readiness to embrace new ways of living that align with God's will. So, we might ask ourselves, do we need to make some changes?

Today, on this significant second Sunday of Advent, we are not just called to reflect, but to act. How ready are we for the Lord's coming? Our readings today, particularly John the Baptist's message, guide this path of readiness, urging us to be prepared and open to the transformative power of God's love. It's not just a journey for us, it's a responsibility. Are we ready to take it on?

In the Gospel, we hear John the Baptist sounding the alarm in his fiery but grace-filled voice, which heralds the coming of the Lord and calls us to prepare our hearts for his arrival during the Advent season. *"Repent ... Prepare the way for the Lord."* (cf Matthew 3:2, 3; cf Mark 1:3; cf Luke 3:4). Repentance, a key aspect of spiritual preparation, involves recognizing our sins, feeling remorse for them, and making a commitment to change our ways. Those words are directed to each of us. Prepare the way for the Lord. *Preparar el camino del Senor.* Are we listening attentively to the one shouting in the desert? What does it say about our relationship with Jesus? *Nos estamos preparando para Cristo?* Are we preparing for Christ?

John the Baptist

When we wake up, let's try this. Look around. Thank God we are inside our homes. And when we are in the Church, thank God we are inside our church. Thank God we are here. Thank God wherever you are. Thank God we are alive. Let us not just prepare for the 'to-do' things, but let us prepare for the greatest gift of all-Christ. Let us be grateful for this opportunity for spiritual growth and reflection that Advent brings.

Wind, rain, and cold spells are around us. Winter is here. Tree leaves are falling. The grounds need sweeping and cleaning. Gardeners and landscapers are getting busy. It is the same with us. As we prepare ourselves for these "to-do" things, are we preparing for Christ?

How do we do this in the coming days? We can begin by reconciling ourselves to God, improving our friendship with Jesus, the Son of God, and listening attentively. Most of the time, we are unaware of what God is doing in and through us. We also know that becoming aware can take a lifetime of listening and discerning. But there is always a beginning. Our baptism, a sacred ritual that marks our initiation into the Christian faith, can attest to this. Baptism is the beginning of an incredible journey.

We can begin by opening ourselves to love others as God has loved us. We can learn to do this with the grace of, as God would have us do it. The saints did it. Each one of us can do it, too. That is why we are here.

Let me make another big note here. In baptism, we are called by name. During baptism, in my homilies, I say to the parents and godparents, and the people of God present this: do you know that God is calling our children and us to sainthood - not only right now, but every day of our lives? Sainthood, a state of being completely united with God, is not reserved for a select few, but is a calling for all Christians. (And I purposely wait a few seconds to elicit their reaction. And I am encouraged when I hear...yes! (from almost everyone present)... and when I see some nodding of heads (...like this...' nodding'...in approval)).

But we are all constantly on a journey, a pilgrimage, and still at it. Our baptism was just the beginning of a purposeful journey toward holiness. And we are not to take it lightly. We must understand that the journey is a life-long process.

Baptism – the beginning of an incredible journey

John the Baptist's cry from the wilderness has echoed through the ages, heralding the transformative nature of Advent. This is a time of change, a time when we learn to celebrate and live out fully who God called us to be. It's a time of living in accordance with God's commandments, showing love and compassion to others, and striving for holiness. We celebrate our faith more intensely through Mass, sacraments, and acts of charity, eagerly anticipating the spiritual growth that awaits us.

The Holy Spirit has been poured into us, and the Spirit of God continues to guide us and the Church. Jesus promised that. Let us take on that promise with a grateful heart. Again, we are at the beginning of an incredible journey, a journey of faith, love, and service, a journey that leads us closer to God and to our true selves.

Prayer: *Let us thank God as we continue with our celebration. Let us also ask for the Almighty God's grace so that this time of our journey renews us in Spirit, and that this advent season leads us to welcome His Son, Jesus, with a joyful heart. Amen.*

CHAPTER 4

Being Generous In Our Little Ways

(Matthew 20:1–16)
(GP: Mark 10:31; Luke 13:30)

Gospel: *"The kingdom of Heaven is like a landowner who went out at dawn to hire laborers for his vineyard. After agreeing with them for the usual daily wage, he sent them into his vineyard. Going out at about nine o'clock, he say others standing in the marketplace, and he said to them, 'You too go into my vineyard and I will give you what is just.' So they went off. [And] he went out again around noon, and around three o'clock, and did likewise. Going out about five o'clock, he found others standing around, and said to them, 'Why do you stand here idle all day?' They answered, 'Because no one has hired us.' He said to them, 'You too, go into my vineyard.' When it was evening the owner of the vineyard said to his foreman, 'Summon the laborers and give them their pay, beginning with the last and ending with the first. When those who had started about five o'clock came, each received the same daily wage. So when the first came, they thought that they would receive more, but each of them also got the usual wage. And on receiving it they grumbled against the landowner, saying, 'These last ones worked only one hour, and you have made them equal to us, who bore the day's burden and heat. He said to one of them in reply, 'My friend, I am not cheating you. Did you*

not agree with me for the usual wage? Take what is yours and go.
What if I wish to give this last one the same as you? [Or] am I not
free to do as I wish with my own money? Are you envious because
I am generous?' Thus, the last will be first, and the first will be
last." (Matthew 20:1-16)

This parable is not a paper on labor relations or a college-level law
degree lesson on providing a just wage for workers. In our world of labor
laws today, this parable would be hard to swallow. It may belong in the
realm of an "unfair labor practice." However, we can look at it more
profoundly, perhaps on a spiritual level. Fr. Paul Holmes wrote:

> "The 'daily wage' Jesus is talking about is really "heaven."
> The whole story is about God giving "heaven" to anyone
> he pleases. What seems unfair is that God seems to be
> offering the same "heaven" to latecomers as he offers to
> those who have been at it from the beginning of the day.
> [...] As Americans, especially, this sounds like heresy.
> Right? Our whole culture is based on the "American
> Dream": that with hard work, and the sweat of your
> brow, you can pull yourself up by your bootstraps and
> become a millionaire! [...]Jesus seems to be saying that
> you and I can come to Mass every Sunday, say our daily
> prayers, and go to novenas; that we can be kind and
> generous to our neighbor; that we can forgive and love
> our enemies, even – and that we'll get the same reward
> as someone who has a deathbed conversion. This flies
> in the face of our sense of justice!"[31]

Our gospel encounter with the Lord today is a profound and awe-
inspiring experience, enriched by the powerful examples he has given us. It
invites us to delve deeply into its meaning and interpretation, challenging
our thoughts and actions, not just for ourselves but also for others.

Upon reading the parable, what struck me was not a lesson on
job worth, employee dedication, or pride in our work. Instead, it was

a profound insight into God's infinite justice, a justice that surpasses human understanding and initiative. This story is a testament to God's wisdom and generosity, often unseen by our worldly eyes, evoking in us a sense of humility and gratitude.

Our Father in Heaven always takes the initiative to spur man into action. As always, He gives us the faculties to discern what is righteous in His loving eyes. One of those faculties is the grace and ability to control what is not pleasing in God's eyes. He is giving us an example of not being passive but active. For instance, He came to John the Baptist to be baptized in the Jordan even though it was not necessary for him to do so. He took the initiative. He did this also to draw us to Himself. He wants us to think for ourselves. Not so much as to rely on others to think for us when it comes to our belief in God. Not to be passive. He wants us to work and exercise our God-given control toward our lives in God, never forgetting to work toward the perpetration of His kingdom as he awaits us to eternal glory in heaven.

These sound like really tall orders for us. Yet, as our ever-loving Father, he also gives us the freedom to realize that we do not have control over everything. There are so many things in this world that we cannot control. Our experience in the last 2,000-plus years can attest to these things. Famine. Disease. Pandemic. Wars. Death. No matter what humans do, we must keep up to the ideal. However, we have also seen signs of God's power in intervening and manifesting His limitless generosity, justice, and love in times of need. We only need to ask Him. That is why He taught us how to pray.

One other thing: "Let go and let God," as the saying goes. God will do the rest if we do our part—work, pray, love God, and love our neighbors as ourselves. If we are willing and open to God's *grace, the* Lord's generosity and justice can be within our grasp.

Prayer: *God our Father, work is your gift to us, a call to reach new heights using our talents for all good. We pray for your grace to help us be generous, loving, forgiving, and giving in our little ways. Never let us astray from your teachings today that your generosity and justice know no limit. May our gratitude to You be by saying "Thank You, Lord" and by acts of generosity to others. Amen.*

CHAPTER 5

Say "Yes" As You Mean It

(Matthew 21:28-32)

Gospel: *What is your opinion? A man had two sons. He came to the first and said, "Son, go out and work in the vineyard today.' He said in reply, 'I will not,' but afterwards he changed his mind and went. The man came to the other son and gave the same order. He said in reply, 'Yes, sir,' but did not go. Which of the two did his father's will?" They answered, "The first." Jesus said to them, "Amen, I say to you, tax collectors and prostitutes are entering the kingdom of God before you. When John came to you in the way of righteousness, you did not believe him; but tax collectors and prostitutes did. Yet even when you saw that, you did not later change your minds and believe him."(Matthew 21:28-32)*

Every Wednesday morning, I drive the church's pantry truck to bring food and groceries to the homeless encampment site near Coyote Creek.

On one of those days, near a local area known as 'the jungle,' we didn't know that two police cars were guarding the entrance to the dirt road that led there. The construction workers just placed two huge boulders as if to fence the gate. No vehicles allowed. They are restricting everyone, even

volunteers like us. They did this for everyone's safety because some maintenance and cleaning were happening. Will they let us in? There were lots of people, street people, and homeless people. The press and a van full of the local News TV crew covered and recorded what was happening.

With my truck stopped in the right lane, I had to decide whether to continue driving while a caravan of volunteer cars followed me. A few of them were already honking, expressing their concern about the situation and urging me to decide. How annoying can that be? What should I do?

I was torn between turning around and going back to the church with all the food in the truck, and the thought of the people depending on us for their food and sustenance. They are hungry and thirsty. I prayed, 'O, Lord, what should I do?' The weight of the situation was heavy on my heart.

One of our lady volunteers was in her car directly behind mine. Looking at her in the back mirror, she signaled me to hold on. I thought she would ask the cops if it was okay for all of us and me to hop over the curb. I was right. She bravely pleaded with the cops to let us go through, explaining the urgency of our mission. Only then were we allowed. I drove the truck and hopped over the curb. And yes, the cops even thanked us we were giving food to the unhoused people who were hungry. That enables us to do our work quickly and distribute the food. Everything went well after that.

As an afterthought, I went and talked to the cops. I thanked them for helping us maintain a good flow of traffic and for understanding our mission. The distribution of the food and groceries went well. Everybody was happy. That morning, I gained two new friends from the police department.

In today's Gospel, Jesus tells a story about afterthoughts. Two young men had second thoughts about their choices. One young man said "yes" and then did not do what he said he would; the other said "no" and did what he said he would not. Jesus asks,

"Which of the two did the will of his father? " Let's look at the possible answers.

> "First is saying 'yes' and acting 'no.' Sometimes people promise and do not perform. [...]We find excuse elsewhere when the sun is hot in the vineyard. A little disappointment or a 'no' to what we want, or a minor disagreement, and we do not show up at the next meeting. In doing so, are we doing the will of the Father?'" [32]

There is a second possibility recognizable in this parable. It is also a hopeful one, thanks be to God:

> "One who says 'no' may later have second thoughts about it and change his mind and say 'yes.' One who has turned to walk away may yet turn around and come back. Well, the way the world is, the way life is, most of us somewhere along the way need to come to a turn-around possibility; we need a change of direction. [...] We are all pilgrims in progress, and we get lost through the night, and in that darkness, we need to go 'the other way.' That 'other way' is to follow the Gospel, to 'do the will of the Father.'" [33]

God knows how difficult it is for us to follow the Gospel and do the will of the Father. Even the saints had a hard time doing this, and we are no exception. So, to help us change our hearts and minds when the time comes, God sends the Word into the world. Christ meets us along the road and joins us in our journey. The Lord sets us in directions we have never gone before. Can we say "yes" to Him?

Today's lesson is a powerful reminder. In all that Jesus teaches us, there's a profound truth-it's never too late to change our ways if we've strayed from God's path. The Lord, ever merciful, is always ready to forgive us. If we approach Him with humility and a contrite heart, we can reconsider our actions. This is especially true if our ultimate aim is to bring greater glory to God and benefit our souls.

Prayer: *Almighty God, we thank You for giving us the strength of will and say "yes" to You. We thank you for allowing us to respond to your will. We pray for your grace to see a vision of your plan for us, especially if we happen to be at the crossroads of our journey. May the word of Christ dwell among us in all its richness. Help us to humble ourselves in your presence always. Amen.*

CHAPTER 6

Thinking Aloud In God

(Matthew 25:14-30)
(GP: Mark 13:34; Luke 19:11-27)

Gospel: *It will be as when a man is going on a journey called in his servants and entrusted his possessions to them. To one he gave five talents; to another, two; to a third, one – to each according to his ability. Then he went away. Immediately the one who receive five talents went and traded with them, and made another five. Likewise, the one who received two, made another two. But the man who received one went off and dug a hole in the ground and buried his master's money. After a long time the master of those servants came back and settled accounts with them. The one who received five talents came forward bringing the additional five. He said, 'Master, you gave me five talents. See, I have made five more.' His master said to him, 'Well done, my good and faithful servant. Since you were faithful in small matters, I will give you great responsibilities. Come, share your master's joy.' [Then] the who had received two talents also came forward and said, 'Master, you gave me two talents. See, I have made two more.' His master said to him, ' Well done, my good and faithful servant. Since you were faithful in small matters, I will give you great responsibilities. Come, share your master's joy.' Then the one who had received one talent came forward and said, 'Master, I knew you were a demanding person, harvesting where you did not plant and gathering where you did not scatter; so out of fear*

I went off and buried your talent in the ground. Here it is back. His master said to him in reply, 'You wicked, lazy servant. So you knew that I harvest where I did not plant and gather where I did not scatter? Should you not then have put my money in the bank so that I could have got it back with interest on my return? Now then! Take the talent from him and give it to one with ten. For to everyone who has, more will be given and he will grow rich; but from the one who has not, even what he has will be taken away. And throw this useless servant into the darkness outside, where there will be wailing and grinding of teeth.' (Matthew 25:14-30)

You must discover the love of God. You must know the love of God. The love of God must be allowed to live deeply into your heart. Do you remember your basic catechism? Why did God create you? To know Him and to love Him so that you will be with Him in heaven. God always has His bountiful graces waiting for us because He loves us so much.

> "One morning, a little girl came running into the house sobbing. 'What's wrong?' her mother asked. Throwing herself into her mother's arms, the little girl cried, 'God doesn't love me anymore. 'That's not true,' said her mother.
>
> 'God loves you more than you can know.'
>
> 'No, he doesn't,' the child kept on crying. 'I know He doesn't because I tried Him with rose petals (remove the petals one at a time while saying) 'He loves me, he loves me not, he loves me, he loves me not...'"[34]

When things align with our desires, we often attribute it to God's presence. Conversely, when circumstances don't favor us, we may feel abandoned by God. However, the love of God is not a game of chance, like the one depicted in this story. It is a steadfast, unwavering love that never falters. God's love for us surpasses our understanding, and we can always rely on it, regardless of the situation.

In every parable, we are called to decipher the symbolism it presents. In this narrative, the Master symbolizes the Savior, and the servants represent the saints. Each saint is uniquely called by God to serve. God has bestowed upon each servant a distinct gift, tailored to their abilities, to be used for His glory and the enrichment of our souls. As St. Paul reminds us, God's gifts are diverse, distributed according to each individual's unique abilities.

Notice that each servant in the story is given talents, which in this context, are not personal skills or abilities, but a monetary measurement. To keep it simple, one talent is equivalent to a bag full of money. The Master expected as much from the one talent as he did from the other servants who were given five or two.

As we delve into the entire narrative, we come to understand that the talents symbolize the opportunities for us to utilize God's *grace*, abilities, or gifts. However, these opportunities are not without responsibility. We are entrusted with the task of using these gifts in a manner that pleases the Master. It's not the quantity of our gifts that holds significance, but rather, how we utilize them. God is not concerned with the magnitude of our abilities or talents, but with our responsible stewardship of them. As the Apostle Paul wrote in another passage of the Bible, *"My grace is sufficient for you, for power is made perfect in weakness."(2 Corinthians 12:9).*

The lesson we can learn from the Gospel is this: "to face our God-given accountability by using our God-given ability to make it fruitful."[35] Are we actively dedicating time to harness our God-given abilities? Are we making a conscious effort? Or are we passively allowing them to lie dormant? Let's not forget the Gospel's reminder today to reject timidity or passiveness, and instead, embrace the gift that God has bestowed upon us.

The third servant failed to recognize that the Master's sole desire is our sincere effort. The Master's love for him is boundless, surpassing his understanding. This same love, this same desire, is extended to each of us. Recall your catechism. Remember your baptism. Recall your birth. Why did God bring you into existence? God brought us into existence to love Him and to serve Him so that we will be with Him in heaven.

Our Savior's love must be the overpowering force that conquers all, including timidity or fear. What the third servant did to himself and his talent was the opposite of exercising our God-given abilities and gifts and the accountability that comes from those gifts. By burying his talent, he not only missed the opportunity to grow and serve, but he also denied the world the blessings that could have come from his use of that talent. He buried his talent; he let it sleep for a long time or die to nothingness.

Why does the Master call the two servants "good and faithful servants?"(cf Matthew 25:21, 23). When entrusted with responsibilities, they do not run off or spend money on themselves. They made it fruitful. They did some thinking and acted in ways that pleased the Lord. The Lord replied to them: "Well done, my good and faithful servant. Since you were faithful in small matters, I will give you great responsibilities. Come, share your master's joy."(Matthew 25: 21, 23).

Imagine that. The Almighty shares his joy with those who are faithful. We can be assured of that. That's why God created us. God provides. God's love for us is a constant, unwavering force that never fails. We only need to open our hearts and minds to discover the depth and breadth of God's love for us. This love is not just for our benefit, but it is also a love that we are called to share with others. God gives us what we need in abundance so we can also provide and share that love with others. Would you accept that challenge?

Let us turn to the Lord, for He is our source of strength and courage. He is the one who can remove the fear that often resides deep within our hearts. With His help, we can use our gifts righteously, celebrating our joy and friendship with Him without hesitation or doubt.

We are also reminded to share the joy God is giving us. God has made an enormous investment in us. Will we dig a hole and bury what God has given us? Or will we put our God-given graces, abilities, or gifts, such as compassion, leadership, or artistic talent, to beneficial use and celebrate our joy for having these graces and sharing them with others? Do we tell ourselves it is time for us to go to work for the sake of the Kingdom?

Prayer: *Good and loving God, we thank You for all the gifts You have given us. Give us the grace to strengthen our will, put our gifts to compelling use, and always be aware of your goodness in whatever we do. Help us proclaim the Good News and share our joy of being given your graces and blessings. Amen.*

CHAPTER 7

The Heart Of Our Faith

*(Wisdom 1:13-15/ 1 Corinthians 8:7,9, 13-15/ **Mark 5:21-43**)*
(GP: Matthew 9:18-26; Luke 8:40-56)

Gospel: When Jesus had crossed again [in the boat] to the other side, a large crowd gathered around him, and he stayed close to the sea. One of the synagogue officials, named Jairus, came forward. Seeing him he fell at his feet and pleaded earnestly with him, saying, "My daughter is at the point of death. Please, come lay your hands on her that she may get well and live." He went off with him, and a large crowd followed him and pressed upon him.

There was a woman afflicted with hemorrhages for twelve years. She had suffered greatly at the hands of many doctors and had spent all that she had. Yet she was not helped but only grew worse. She had heard about Jesus and came up behind him in the crowd and touched his cloak. She said, "If I but touch his clothes, I shall be cured." Immediately her flow of blood dried up. She felt in her body that she was healed of her affliction. Jesus, aware at once that power had gone out from him, turned around in the crowd and asked, "Who has touched my clothes?" But his disciples said to him, "You see how the crowd is pressing upon you, and yet you asked, "Who touched me?"" And he looked around to see who had done it. The woman, realizing what had happened to her, approached in fear and trembling. She fell down before Jesus and told him the truth. He said to her, "Daughter, your faith has saved you. Go in peace and be cured of your affliction."

While he was still speaking, people from the synagogue official's house arrived and said, "Your daughter has died; why trouble the teacher any longer?" Disregarding the message that was reported, Jesus said to the synagogue official, "Do not be afraid; just have faith." He did not allow anyone to accompany him inside except Peter, James, and John, the brother of James. When they arrived at the house of the synagogue official, he caught sight of a commotion, people weeping and wailing loudly. So he went in and said to them, "Why this commotion and weeping? The child is not dead but asleep." And they ridiculed him. Then he put them all out. He took along the child's father and mother and those who were with him and entered the room where the child was. He took the child by the hand and said to her, "Talitha koum," which means, "Little girl, I say to you, arise!" The girl, a child of twelve, arose immediately and walked around. [At that] they were utterly astounded. He gave strict orders that no one should know this and said that she should be given something to eat. (Mark 5:21-43)

One late afternoon in the hospital, I visited and prayed with a woman about to undergo cancer surgery. The surgery will happen in the morning after. Her husband was there, and from the looks of his face, I knew there was so much doubt as to how the surgery would turn out. When I entered her room, I saw peace and contentment on her face. What a contrast! She held my hand during prayer. I felt so peaceful while praying with her.

After we ended our prayer, she said, "You know, I don't worry. I have trust in God."

What can I say in response to that? There was so much humility and sincerity in those words form her. I believed her. What a tremendous amount of faith this woman had! I felt like she was ready for anything.

I then went to the next room after. Next to the woman's room was another patient. The man already lost one of his legs because of diabetes and is due for another surgery. He asked me to help him pray the moment I entered. I did not even have the time to introduce myself.

Due to other major illnesses, he is now crippled not only physically but also mentally. But he was not worried or showing any sign of fear or loneliness. Amazing! He said that because he is in the hospital, he no longer feels alone and helpless. When I asked him to tell me more, he said he placed his life in God's hands. Faith and trust in the compassion of God, who cares for him in spirit has carried him in these troubling times.

The two stories before us from the Gospel today, speaks of trust in the compassionate healing of Jesus.[36] In the first Gospel story, the woman who suffered from bleeding for 12 years approached Jesus with fear and trembling but with a firm thought that Jesus had the power to heal her. She could touch his garment. Then, she will be cured of her sickness. What's going on in this story?

Trust. The woman was deemed by the people in those days to be unclean. If we had been there, we would have experienced surprise, even shock - that Jesus would heal this woman or think that this woman would even come close to where Jesus was. We could come up with a question similar to the question in the mind of Jesus' disciples: do you think that Jesus will heal you because you touched his clothes? Surprise! Jesus does just that. The woman trusted. Do we trust Jesus in the same way? In our own lives, we may face situations that seem impossible to overcome, but Jesus' compassionate healing is not limited by our circumstances. He invites us to trust in his power and love, just as the woman did. God wants us to have the right ideas about him. We need trust in our hearts. Trust in Jesus. Trust is the heart of our faith.

In the 1st story in the Gospel, where the 12-year-old girl died, we see trust at work again. As the leader of the local synagogue, Jairus knew it was dangerous to have anything to do with Jesus. Yet, upon seeing Jesus, he fell on his feet and pleaded earnestly with Jesus. The leader trusted in Jesus. And Jesus did more. Jesus raised the element of compassion that carries over to situations of death. He said something difficult for us to understand even today. He gives a more profound meaning of death. This story offers us a powerful lesson about trust and compassion.

Listen. Last night, we all went to sleep. But this morning, we woke up to a new day—a new perspective on life. This is a metaphor for the spiritual awakening that Jesus brings. We fall asleep in one place (here on earth), where we are often bound by our physical and societal limitations, and wake up in another (heaven), where we are free to experience the fullness of God's love and compassion. In the second story, the young girl wakes up. The first face she sees is the compassionate face of Jesus, welcoming her into this new reality.

Our prayers, dear brothers and sisters, are that someday, by the power of God and the compassion of Jesus, we will see Jesus' face and receive eternal life with God. This is not just a hope for the future, but a present reality that we can experience through our faith and trust in Jesus' compassionate healing.

In both stories, Jesus demonstrated a level of compassion and love that was beyond human comprehension. He saw the need, and his compassion and love took over. Both were daughters, and both were dying. Yet, Jesus did more than heal them physically. He returned life to both. Jesus returned the girl to Jairus and her family, restoring their joy and hope. Jesus healed the woman and returned her to her community, giving her a new way of life. His actions were not just about physical healing, but about restoring dignity, hope, and community. He gave them a new lease on life.

When we talk about illness or death, we often find ourselves grappling with questions that our human minds cannot fully grasp or accept. The Gospel stories we are exploring today offer some insights into these profound mysteries. They remind us that there is a limit to our knowledge, and that faith is not about having all the answers, but about trusting in God's wisdom and love. When we pray, the challenge is to trust in God, who is the source of everything we ask for, even when we don't fully understand his ways.

The stories I shared with you and the Gospel narrative all converge on one central theme: trust in the love and compassionate healing of Jesus. The message is clear-we are called to open our hearts and trust in God. As we navigate our human lives, we are to live them in faith, trusting in the Son of God who loves us and gave himself for us. This is our path-a life of faith, compassion, and prayer. In this path, we find comfort and peace, knowing that our trust in God will guide us through life's challenges.

Prayer: *Almighty Father, with a humble and contrite heart, we ask for your grace to give us a new life free from sin. Teach us always to be able to turn to your Son, our Lord Jesus, without fear in all our afflictions, trusting in Him in any situation that He is with us. May the word of Christ dwell among us in all its richness. O Holy Spirit, help us be strong in faith and love. Amen.*

CHAPTER 8

God Gives Us The Grace To Accomplish Our Mission

(Mark 6: 7-13)
(GP: Matthew 9:35; Luke 9:1-6)

Gospel: *He summoned the Twelve and began to send them out two by two and gave them authority over unclean spirits. He instructed them to take nothing for the journey but a walking stick - no food, no sack, no money in their belts. They were, however, to wear sandals but not a second tunic. He said to them, "Wherever you enter a house, stay there until you leave from there. Whatever place does not welcome you or listen to you, leave there and shake the dust off your feet in testimony against them." So they went off and preached repentance. They drove out many demons, and they anointed with oil many who were sick and cured them. (Mark 6:7-13)*

We often encounter words that challenge us, prompting us to consider our next move. In these moments, we have the opportunity to grow personally. We ponder whether our actions could enhance our lives, improve our relationships with family, friends, or co-workers, or perhaps reveal areas where we can strive for more.

Jesus sends the apostles out two by two. We wonder why. Security in numbers? No. For convenience's sake? Yes. And for practical purposes, too. One apostle can help the other in times of need, like when they must look for food or find a water source to quench their thirst. However, the real reason is that each apostle can draw strength from the other. When one perhaps shows weakness in spirit, the other can help. Then, they can focus more on their mission.

Jesus instructed them to take nothing to their mission but a walking stick, a tunic, and a pair of sandals – no food, no sack, no money. They were to preach repentance, anoint, and heal.

Just as the apostles had a mission, so do we. Today, that mission and the challenging words we face are enormous. We can only do so much with the essentials of food or money. We must not simply rely on the goodness of others, but share collectively and as a community in the same mission. The question is: are we focused on them? Are we all united in fulfilling the mission? Are we drawing strength from each other? This unity and shared purpose can give us a sense of belonging and a greater sense of purpose.

> "In the movie Apollo 13, [...]the three astronauts were on a mission. But they are not alone in that mission. Everyone at mission command is part of the mission as well. Each person, whether on board or in the command center, has a specific part of the mission to complete. Each person is focused entirely on the mission. We as believers are on a mission for God. We each are responsible for our personal part in that mission. When we discover what that personal mission is, we must give it our focus [...]"[37]

What do we need to focus on our mission in the Church? Today's Gospel answers this question: the walking stick, the tunic, the pair of sandals, and, of course, ourselves as followers of Jesus Christ. Let's look at what the apostles had as Jesus commanded them.

Their walking stick is God's way of manifesting His dominion over anything that will come in the way of his mission. And so do we. We have God's blessing. We have God's grace. Have you ever wondered how God helps us when we are on a mission for the Church? Our walking stick held tightly in our hand- raised toward heaven in prayer, planted firmly on the ground each step of our journey, is God's word that He is with us always. God is in our midst when we are gathered in his name or fulfilling a mission for Him. Walking with Jesus and discovering God's love keeps us from falling into doubt, helplessness, ignorance, and uncertainty. For us, that's the power of prayer.

The apostles have their tunics. We have them, too. The tunic protects us from fear, our shield against the corruption threatening our faith.

Just as the apostles had their sandals, we also have them. These sandals are not just a physical protection, but a symbol of our community. They shield us from the rocky path and guard us in case we step into the thorns along the way. As we walk through the valley of tears, challenges, and death through sin, our brothers and sisters and our community are our companions in our journey. We walk with Jesus, and Jesus walks with us. Let us not focus on human weakness or limitations but depend on God to make our ministries fruitful. Like the disciples, we have the power to cast out selfishness.

Christ has prepared us for everything we need. He has given us his grace, a divine gift that we can always rely on. If we ask for His blessing to do good for the sake of others, He will not hesitate to give His blessing to us, for he loves us. He taught us to trust in Him. He prepared us to help each other, especially those who are poor and losing hope. Let us help each other accomplish our mission to proclaim and live the Gospel, knowing that His grace and blessing are always with us.

When we were baptized, Jesus called us by name. Our priest blesses us after every mass. We are also blessed each time we pray the Liturgy of the Hours, saying, "May the Lord bless us, forgive our sins, and lead us to life everlasting." And we sign ourselves with the sign of the cross to acknowledge God's gift of blessing for us.

Prayer: *Almighty Father, we ask for your grace to help us see and focus on our mission for the Church, protect us from what could harm us, lead us to what will save us from eternal damnation, and bring us closer to You through prayer. Amen.*

CHAPTER 9

The Freedom To Lean On Our Fears In The WORD

(Mark 10:17-30)
(GP: Matthew 19:16-30; Luke 18:18-30)

Gospel: *As he was setting out on a journey, a man ran up, knelt down before him, and asked him, "Good teacher, what must I do to inherit eternal life?" Jesus answered him, "Why do you call me good? No one is good but God alone. You know the commandments: You shall not kill; you shall not commit adultery; you shall not steal; you shall not bear false witness; you shall not defraud; honor your father and your mother.'" He replied and said to him, "Teacher, all of these I have observed from my youth." Jesus, looking at him, loved him and said to him, "You are lacking in one thing. Go, sell what you have, and give to [the] poor and you will have treasure in heaven; then come, follow me." At that statement his face fell, and he went away sad, for he had many possessions.*

Jesus looked around and said to his disciples, "How hard it is for those who have wealth to enter the kingdom of God!" The disciples were amazed at his words. So Jesus again said to them in reply, "Children, how hard it is to enter the kingdom of God! It is easier for a camel to pass through [the] eye of [a] needle than for one who is rich to enter the kingdom of God." They were exceedingly astonished and said among themselves, "Then who can be saved?" Jesus looked at them and said, "For human beings, it is impossible, but not for God." Peter began to say to him, "We have given up everything and followed you." Jesus said, "Amen, I say to you, there is no one who have given up house or brothers or sisters or mother or father or children or lands for my sake and for the sake of the gospel who will not receive a hundred times more now in the present age: houses and brothers and sisters and mothers and children and lands, with persecutions, and eternal life in the age to come." (Mark 10:17-30)

The humility and goodness of the man in this Gospel is so touching that *"Jesus looking at him, loved him." (cf Mark 10:21).* People call this story "the story of the rich, young man." I like to believe that the "rich, young man" is humble. I imagine the man's sadness was not the story's culmination but rather a beginning. As often happens, life allows everyone to respond in ways we can embrace. God, in his love for us, gives us such freedom. Even to lean on our fears in Him. God gives us many chances to respond to our call, follow Him, and be good children and disciples of Jesus. While those opportunities are left open to us, it is up to us to respond. While Jesus looks at us lovingly, he opens to us, allowing us to approach and lean on him.

What is the key lesson we can draw from these passages? It is the understanding that God is not distant or unapproachable, but rather, he is always within reach, open to our embrace, and ready to support us. We can lean on him without hesitation.

Our Lord and Savior, Jesus Christ, serves as our High Priest, interceding on our behalf. We were reminded of this at the start of the Mass when, as your deacon, I led us in the Penitential Act. Jesus, seated at the right hand of the Father, intercedes for us. His prayers for us should embolden us to approach the throne of grace with confidence. As the inspired writer of Hebrews tells *us, we should 'confidently approach the throne of grace to receive mercy and to find grace for timely help.'* How can we not find the grace that is being offered to us? How can we not accept the grace of God? What is wrong with us?

Life is brutal and sometimes cruel. We experience shock and sadness.

THE WORD IS WITH US

Not everything is peachy. Where do we turn to during those times? We approach the throne of *grace to receive mercy* in humility and sincerity, prayerfully and confidently.

The second thing we learn about God is that He is merciful. *Mesiricordes Pater Noster.* God, our Father is full of mercy and compassion. This should fill us with hope and relief, knowing that no matter our weaknesses or struggles, God's nature is love. We have Jesus, who intimately knows our situation and understands our cares. The Word is with us, offering us comfort and solace.

Here is a story:

> "There was a memorable scene between Matt Damon (playing the down and out golfer Rannulf Junuh attempting to recover his once fantastic golf game and his previous way of life), and Will Smith (as Bagger Vance, Junuh's caddy). Junuh was losing his game in this golf tournament against Bobby Jones and Walter Hagen. Junuh got himself in the thick of the woods, all by himself, not confident in how to hit the ball out from there, and safely land into the fairways. At that moment, Junuh had a flashback of his past life, with his own demons battling inside of himself. [...] He wanted to quit right there, and just walk away. But Bagger issued a challenge for Junuh, to use his gift of freedom to rid himself of what was keeping him from his authentic self.
>
> Looking lovingly at him like a father, Bagger said: 'you have a choice. Time for you to choose. Come out of your shadows.' And in a moment of overwhelming emotion, Junuh says, 'I can't.' But Bagger, still looking lovingly at him says, 'Yes you can. You are not alone. I am right here with you. I have been here all along. Now play your game. The one that was meant for you when you came into this world. Take your chance. Take your shot. Give it your everything.'"[38]

You know the rest of the story. Junuh found the freedom to lean on his fear. However, he did not have any idea at first. But the Word was with him. He was looking at him like God looks at us - lovingly. God allows us to find Him amidst the hazards of uncertainties, the forest of doubts, and fears and lean on Him to eliminate all our discontent and worries. God makes known to us His Word. And God sees us, through Christ, as if we are without blemish. He meets us where we are. Even when we are alone, He is present in us. We do not have to go far.

Prayer: *As we come to the table of the Lord who looks at us always so lovingly and mercifully, let us thank Him and ask for His grace to help us to never doubt that He is with us always, that He keeps us always in that loving embrace, and for us to be able to receive Him, with joy, praise, and thanksgiving. Amen.*

CHAPTER 10

We Are In God's Hands

(Luke 2:22-40)

THE HOLY FAMILY OF JESUS, MARY, and JOSEPH

Gospel: *When the days were completed for their purification according to the law of Moses, they took him up to Jerusalem to present him to the Lord, "Every male that opens the womb shall be consecrated to the Lord," and to offer the sacrifice of "a pair of turtledoves or two young pigeons," in accordance with the dictate of the law of the Lord.*

Now there was a man in Jerusalem whose name was Simeon. This man was righteous and devout, awaiting the consolation of Israel, and the holy Spirit was upon him. It had been revealed to him by the holy Spirit that he should not see death before he had seen the Messiah of the Lord. He came in the Spirit into the temple; and when the parents brought in the child Jesus to perform the custom of the law in regard to him, he took him into his arms and blessed God, saying:

"Now, Master, you may let your servant go in peace, according to your word, for my eyes have seen your salvation, which you prepared in sight of all the peoples, a light for the revelation to the Gentiles, and glory for your people Israel."

The child's father and mother were amazed at what was said about him; and Simeon blessed them and said to Mary his mother, "Behold, this child is destined for the fall and rise of many in Israel, and to be a sign that will be contradicted (and you yourself a sword will pierce) so that the thoughts of many hearts may be revealed. There was also a prophetess, Anna, the daughter of Phanuel, of the tribe of Asher. She was advanced in years, having lived seven years with her husband after her marriage, and then as a widow until she was eighty-four. She never left the temple, but worshipped night and day with fasting and prayer. And coming forward at that very time, she gave thanks to God and spoke about the child to all who were awaiting the redemption of Israel.

When they had fulfilled all the prescriptions of the law of the Lord, they returned to Galilee, to their own town of Nazareth. The child grew and became strong, filled with wisdom; and the favor of God was upon him. (Luke 2:22-40)

The Gospel of Luke today unveils a profoundly sacred event in the life of a young couple, Mary and Joseph, embarking on a pilgrimage from Galilee to Jerusalem to consecrate their child to God. This act, familiar to many of us who have children or grandchildren, carries a weight of significance that can shape a lifetime of profound memories with our loved ones.

Central to this event are two prophets, Simeon and Anna, who, inspired by the Holy Spirit, proclaimed that the child is "salvation..." and that God's promises are now fulfilled in the child of Mary and Joseph. Simeon's prophetic words, *"a sword will pierce Mary's own soul,"* add a poignant layer to the narrative.

As a family man, I understand the challenges of modern family life. The Gospel offers us some valuable lessons in this regard. Allow me to share a captivating story I came across that I believe will resonate with you:

> "A father and his 7-year-old son one sunny day, were at a nearby park, just lying on the grass, looking at the sky and watching the clouds float gently overhead. Well, they just stopped there after dropping off the mother at the mall, for some "after Christmas" shopping. You know, 70% off on lots of stuff.

After a few minutes of silence, the boy turned to the father and asked, 'Dad, why are we here?' The father was philosophical. 'That's a good question, son. I think we are here to enjoy days like this, to experience nature in all its glory, the vast sky, the beauty of the trees, the birds singing. [...]We are here to celebrate life – passing your school exams, the birth of a new member of the family, promotion at work. We are here to comfort those dearest to us in times of distress, provide kindness and compassion, to let them know that no matter how bad a situation may seem, they are not alone. Does that answer your question, son?'

'Not really, Dad,' the boy answered.

'No?', asked the father.

'No, the son replied. 'What I meant was, why are we here, when Mom said to pick her up 35 minutes ago?'"[39]

Kids say the most delightful things! The world is already brimming with God's grace, and it overflows with the innocent charm of children. Their words and actions have a magical way of making our troubles fade into the background. They can even inspire us to embrace their playful spirit as our own.

And yet, having them in your life or having a family is also not the easiest thing. The parents of our Lord also faced challenges in life. For example, they had to settle for a pair of turtledoves, which was a common offering for those who couldn't afford a lamb for sacrifice. This was a clear indication of their financial struggles in those times. Of course, those times were different than ours today. And yet, sometimes we ask why God doesn't make it easier for us financially. If God were going to help anyone with their finances, it would have been Mary and Joseph. What about you and me? What about others facing the same challenges as Mary and Joseph did?

Perhaps there are certain aspects of parenting that God leaves for us to discover. Maybe God wants us to realize that there are more valuable gifts we can offer our children than material wealth – our time, our attention, our moral compass, and spiritual guidance.

That's one lesson. Mary and Joseph couldn't surround their child with material goods, but they could cover Him with love, time, attention, and spiritual and moral guidance. Even though He is the Son of God, let us remember he was a real boy. He needed the love and nurture of a family. Every child does. Every one of our children does—even you and me. No matter who we are or where we come from, the love and care we give to our children is what truly matters.

But here is another lesson. Mary and Joseph had no idea what lay ahead. They were not just facing financial challenges, but also societal pressures, political unrest, and the constant fear for their child's safety. Mary and Joseph could only look forward to a picture-perfect, charmed life in the Christmas story. They just tried to survive and to make ends meet, perhaps just like us. They could not see where God was leading their son. Only after His resurrection did Mary comprehend.

When a child is born, we have no idea what the future may hold. No matter how old the child is, there's plenty to worry about. Parenting is a journey filled with unexpected twists and turns, and it's our love and dedication that guide us through these uncertainties.

When I was growing up, my mom told me about their sacrifices in raising us, all seven surviving children at that time (they had eleven children, including me; four died during their infancy or at very early ages). She told me stories about them to give examples when I had done something wrong or ignored things that mattered to her. I learned my lessons the hard way. I remember her profound words whenever I struggled with challenges within my own family, even after I got married. My mom tells me, "Son, you will fully realize how much sacrifice your parents made for you when you become a parent yourself and raise your children. I forgive you. I love you. I am always here if you need me. I am always praying for you." I recalled that my parents had to work 24/7 to pay for their children's school fees. I recall how that made me appreciate the value of hard work and sacrifice.

The Family of Jesus, Mary and Joseph

Standing on the threshold of a new calendar year, we know only one thing. Mary and Joseph knew the same thing: *that we- and those we love- are in God's hands.* This means we rely totally on God's providence, which can provide us with comfort and guidance as we navigate the uncertainties of the new year.

That doesn't mean life will always be a smooth road for us. We all encounter bumps along the road, some so high it takes time and sacrifice before we can get over them. But we do not give up because we trust that the unseen hand of Christ is leading us. We let the peace of Christ control our hearts. In God's grace is our peace. We let the ever-merciful God enable us to forgive one another. We ask God to help us put on love because love is the bond that unites us toward perfection. Love is what God asks of us, in Christ Jesus.

Before we see the light of day tomorrow, remember to bless this passing year for all our experiences. Let us not forget – all we found and all we lost. The change we see tomorrow will only be the date on the calendar unless we let go of what weighs us down today. To do this, we can offer our prayers to God. We can do good things for other people. Remember all our blessings this past year, and be grateful to God. Also, remember the things that did not go well, if possible. We can learn from them. The lesson is that we must try not to repeat those mistakes.

My brothers and sisters, just as this day was significant for the Holy Family of Jesus, we can also do the same – making this day and tomorrow more important for ourselves and for our church . The Holy Family of Jesus can be our guide. We can strive to know God more intimately so that we can love God more dearly, follow Him more closely, and give our share in helping a love-starved world. We can try to do all these things. The rest is in the hands of God. Let us remember the Holy Family of Jesus, and let them be our guide. Amen.

May you all have a Blessed New Year!

Prayer: *Jesus, eternal Word of the Father, You made yourself subject to Mary and Joseph. In the family at Nazareth, You grew in wisdom, age, and grace before God and men and women; help us to grow in all things toward You. Teach us humility and make us attentive to your word. Let us also ponder your words in hearts that are pure and good. Enable us to be like your Mother, who is also our Mother, who ponders your words in hearts that are obedient and full of love. We pray for your grace to enable us to always pray for our children, including those children who have no one to pray for them. Amen.*

CHAPTER 11

Today You Will Be With Me In Paradise

(Luke 23:43).

Gospel: *He replied to him, "Amen, I say to you, today you will be with me in Paradise." (Luke 23:43)*

This one-line verse in the Gospel is so simple yet full of meaning. From the cross, Christ made a promise to a man we know as the Good Thief. Tradition has given him a name, Dismas. The one who cried: ...*Jesus, remember me when you come into your kingdom (Luke 23:42).* Jesus answered Dismas and made a promise that echoes God's eternal love and mercy.

The 7th commandment, *"You shall not steal" (Exodus 20:15),* expresses the action that Dismas disregarded or ignored. Instead of earning his livelihood through honest labor, he gave himself to brigandry and thievery. These crimes were commonplace in 1st-century Palestine and are still common today in many parts of the world. Even today, it is so easy to live a life of want and desire: stealing, disordered desire, and coveting other people's property and money.

Christ turns to one of these scoundrels, Dismas, and says, *"Amen, I say to you, today you will be with me in Paradise" (Luke 23:43).* Christ utters a great mystery of divine providence to Dismas. Why Dismas and not the other man? Is there any explanation for this sudden reversal of eternal life for Dismas? Because of this mystery, isn't there also hope for us? Let us ponder about that for a moment. Our God forgives. He is the Ever Merciful Father. Dismas with a simple prayer asked only to remember him. This mystery of divine providence invites us to reflect on our own spiritual journey and the hope it holds. It shows us that no matter our past, forgiveness can transform our future.

We can learn from Dismas. We can learn not to give up even in the worst of conditions. Christ heard what Dismas said to the other thief. *"Have you no fear of God for you are subject to the same condemnation?... the sentence we received corresponds to our crimes." (Luke 23:40-41).* Perhaps unbeknownst to Dismas, that was a profound supplication for the Father.

What led Dismas to turn to Christ and seek his mercy and forgiveness? It was not just his total surrender, but also the faith that God had instilled in him. This faith was evident in his actions, as he responded to the call of Jesus. It is a reminder to us that when we are blessed, when the Spirit moves us, we should respond with faith and action.

We are being reminded that God is the ever-gentle and loving God. Salvation is freely given. You see, God allows us to make a choice. Only one of those crucified with Jesus receives the promise. Dismas acted on the truth with the humility that even a thief can give. Dismas had to have been moved by the Spirit to seek forgiveness, and he had desired so much to receive it. What else could have pushed him? This is the generosity of God's mercy and love, offering us the opportunity to deepen our relationship with Jesus. It's a reminder that God's love is unconditional, always there for us, no matter our past or present.

Dismas was seeking not a place but a relationship- mercy and love. Are we seeking a relationship with Jesus? Are we pursuing his passion for us in drawing us to Him?

The kingdom of God is where love reigns- love in the truth. In Galatians, St. Paul reminded people that what matters for our eternal happiness, beatitude, and entrance to Paradise, the Kingdom of God, is faith- God's truth – working through love *(cf. Galatians 5:6).*

Faith, hope, and love. Dismas did not need a physical space, but an order of love without blemish. His transformation was marked by a simple act of kindness toward Jesus that overcame selfishness. In doing so he showed something good that conquered evil. He was honest and sincere. Jesus, in his infinite love, opened Paradise for the thief who believed in Him and desired forgiveness. This is a powerful testament to the love and mercy of our God, and it offers us the opportunity to deepen our relationship with Jesus.

The answer is clear: "God wants us to recognize ourselves in the Good Thief. God knows that we are weak. But God wants us to know that whatever we did to depart from his saving plan, we can still cry out to Jesus.

Prayer: *Lord Jesus, we cry out to You. Turn your head lovingly toward us. We are weak. Help us not lose hope and never cease to pray so that we will be with You in paradise someday. We desire forgiveness, too. Grant us your mercy, forgive our sins, and remit their punishment. Have mercy on us poor souls. Have mercy, Lord. Have mercy.*

CHAPTER 12

Encountering Jesus

*(Acts 10:3a, 37-43/ 1 Corinthians 5:6b – 8/ **Luke 24:13-35**)*
(GP: Mark 16:12-13)

Easter Sunday (Afternoon Mass)

Gospel: *Now that very day two of them were going to a village seven miles from Jerusalem called Emmaus, and they were conversing about all the things that had occurred. And it happened that while they were conversing and debating, Jesus himself drew near and walked with them, but their eyes were prevented from recognizing him. He asked them, "What are you discussing as you walk along?" They stopped, looking downcast. One of them named Cleopas, said to him in reply. "Are you the only visitor to Jerusalem who does not know of the things that have taken place there in these days?" And he replied to them, "What sort of things?" They said to him, "The things that happened to Jesus the Nazarene, who was a prophet mighty in deed and word before God and the people, how our chief priests and rulers both handed him over to a sentence of death and crucified him. But we were hoping that he would be the one to redeem Israel; and besides all these, it is now the third day since this took place. Some women from our group, however, have astounded us: they were at the tomb early in the morning and did not find his body; they came back and reported that they have indeed seen a vision of angels who announced that he was alive. Then some of those with us went to the tomb and found things just as the women had described, but him they did not see." And he said to them, "Oh, how foolish you are! How slow of heart to believe all that the prophets spoke! Was it not necessary that the Messiah should suffer these things and enter into his glory?" Then beginning with Moses and all the prophets, he interpreted to them what referred to him in all the scriptures. As they approached the village to which they were going, he gave the impression that he was going on farther. But they urged him, "Stay with us, for it is nearly evening and the day is almost over." So he went in to stay with them. And it happened that while he was with them at table, he took bread, said the blessing, broke it, and gave it to them. With that their eyes were opened and they recognized him, but he vanished from their sight. Then they said to each other, "Were not our hearts burning [within us] while he spoke to us on the way and opened the scriptures to us?" So they set out at once and returned to Jerusalem where they found gathered together the eleven and those with them who were saying, "The Lord has truly been raised and has appeared to Simon!" Then the two recounted what had taken place on the way and how he was made known to them in the breaking of the bread. (Luke 24:13-35)*

If you have seen the movie *"Risen"* like I did recently, it is an Easter story seen through the eyes of an ordinary Roman soldier.[40] There is a striking similarity between the encounter of the two disciples with Jesus in this Gospel and that of Clauvius Aquila, the Roman soldier in the movie. The encounter happened near the end when Clauvius, a skeptic, utterly confused Tribune, a leader unable to understand how Jesus rose from the dead, found Jesus in the flesh after the resurrection. He saw him – eating and drinking and having fun with his apostles. He also saw him healing a poor leper. From that moment of encounter, the whole world opened up for Clauvius. He became a changed man.

The Gospel today speaks so clearly of the one primary aim of every Gospel– an encounter with Jesus Christ. In every such encounter is another aim – to proclaim and live out the Gospel to the best that we can and with God's *grace*.

At its core, we learn that this is called Evangelization. In today's modern world, Pope Francis has taken the concept of Evangelization to another level. He is challenging us to rethink how we proclaim the Good News. The Holy Father uses all the tools, including social media, to inform and live out the Gospel. He does this in simple, meaningful new ways by preaching, not abstract theology but using simple, clear words to interpret and connect our lives through the Word of God proclaimed. He uses the power of his presence for the common good.

In today's Gospel, we see a larger story that Jesus wants to remind us of. He is showing us how to be witnesses of His presence in us.

First, to be a witness, we need *to see*. We need to keep our eyes, ears, and hearts open. One of my favorite pictures of the Holy Father that appeared on social media was during his first visit to the United States as Pope in 2015.[41]

When the Pope arrived in Philadelphia for a public event, as they headed for downtown, as he waved at the thousands of people lining the runway, all of a sudden, he told his driver to stop the car. Was there something wrong? No. The Pope saw something. Or, he had seen someone. The Holy Father quickly exited his vehicle and crossed a rope line. He approached a mother with a little boy in a wheelchair. The Pope bent down to kiss the boy, exchanged a word or two with the mother, and offered a blessing. The mother, in the midst of the crowd, could only stand there in gratitude and joy.

This powerful display of empathy and care brings me to my second point: the essence of being a witness is in the 'encounter.' The Pope, a firm believer in this principle, often reiterates, 'We must meet others where they are, not where we wish them to be.' This simple yet profound statement encapsulates the Pope's approach to empathy and care.[42]

During one meeting with prisoners, he told them of that memorable encounter at the Last Supper, when Jesus washed his disciples' feet. How many of us remember when the Pope himself – as he was washing the feet adjusted his priest's stole so it wouldn't get wet and turned it instead into a *deacon's* stole.[43] This symbolic gesture resonated deeply with deacons worldwide, reaffirming their crucial roles as servants of the Word and the importance of extending a helping hand whenever possible.

The Pope's words echoed with a profound truth: "the Lord goes in search of us; to all of us he stretches out a helping hand so that we can continue on our journey. Jesus still walks out to the streets… He fills us with hope…boundless hope."[44] These words, filled with the promise of Jesus' eternal presence and boundless hope, are a beacon of light for all.

Brothers and sisters, let us reflect on the profound transformation that faith can bring. In the movie, when Clauvius witnessed a man breaking bread with his apostles, he was enlightened to the fact that it was Jesus our Lord Himself. This was a moment of divine *grace*, a testament to the power of unwavering faith. Despite his initial doubts, Clauvius opened his heart, allowing the grace of curiosity and truth to find him.

Today's Gospel story of the two disciples breaking bread in Galilee serves as a powerful reminder of the importance of being present and attentive. The road to Emmaus teaches us to be mindful, even in the midst of our anxieties and hurts. It reminds us that Jesus may come to us unexpectedly, even on the roads we least expect. The voice we may not hear in the moment may later ignite a fire in our hearts.

Whether we find ourselves in the shoes of Clauvius in the movie or Cleopas and the other disciples in today's gospel, we are reminded to remain peaceful amid oblivion, patient amid doubt, and hopeful on the lonely road of discouragement. Jesus, in His boundless love, will never allow us to be far from Him if we hold onto our faith amid despair— finding joy in Christ, not doubts and distress. Our hearts will be filled with satisfaction if we embrace the opportunity to be transformed by His grace.

Prayer: *God our Father, creator of all, today is a day full of hope and joy. You opened our eyes to what the scriptures foretold: the death and resurrection of our Lord Jesus Christ. May the risen Lord breathe on our minds and open our eyes always so that we will recognize him in the breaking of the bread and follow him in his risen life. Grant this through Christ our Lord. Amen.*

PART FOUR

WE ARE CALLED TO TELL THE STORY

"What was from the beginning, what we have heard, what we have seen with our eyes, what we looked upon and touched with our hands concerns the Word of life – for the life was made visible; we have seen it and testify to it and proclaim to you the eternal life that was made with the Father and was made visible to us – what we have seen and heard we proclaim now to you, so that you too may have fellowship with us; for our fellowship is with the Father and with his Son, Jesus Christ. We are writing this so that our joy may be complete."
– 1 John 1-4

I have my own story. You have your own as well as your friends and colleagues. We all have stories to tell. Stories are stories, yet there are many kinds. But it is different when we are called to tell the story about God. First, it is not easy to tell a story about God. However, we are not alone in this task. Second, the Lord has promised us the Holy Spirit, who will guide us in our storytelling. Through the Holy Spirit's assistance and our desire to pray for our salvation and that of others, it is possible even to tell stories about God. As in Luke 1:37, *"... for nothing will be impossible for God."* With the indwelling of the Holy Spirit, we are stirred to tell the story of our salvation and become part of it.

Through the parables of our Lord Jesus and the myriad stories from the Bible, we are called to proclaim the saving message of the immense love and mercy that our Father has poured into all of humanity. The life of Jesus Christ, from his humble birth to his ultimate sacrifice on the cross and glorious resurrection, holds the power to transform our lives. It is through his life that we find hope, redemption, and the promise of eternal salvation.

We can also give our share and extend our help to those in need to the best of our God-given abilities to help make our fragile world a better place. We can help bring Jesus Christ to anyone who is open to his saving grace. In so doing, we become a part of that story of salvation that can transform the world.

Prayer: *Lord Jesus, help us and be our guide so that we become part of your story of great love and mercy. May your words dwell among us in all their richness. Through your grace, enable us to proclaim your saving message always so that we can do our share in bringing you closer to all people. Thereby, we can also help transform this world with you. Amen.*

CHAPTER 1

Our Gifts To God

(Matthew 2:1–2)

Gospel: *When Jesus was born in Bethlehem of Judea, in the days of King Herod, behold, magi from the east arrived in Jerusalem, saying, "Where is the newborn king of the Jews? We saw his star at its rising and have come to do him homage." (Matthew 2:1-2)*

When I first heard the word *epiphany,* I thought it was one of those funny words.

Consulting with my good friend Webster, who sometimes sits with me, it took me a few tries before I got the pronunciation right. My friend laughs at me whenever I mess up my English. If only my friend could talk, we can always exchange pleasantries. It would be fantastic for everyone. *"Epiphaneia"* is a Greek word that means appearance. For us, it is the manifestation of the divine nature of Christ to the Gentiles as represented by the Magi. God wanted us to know that what we see in that manifestation is God in the flesh, too.

> "In a wondrous act of humility, God shows himself to us as a vulnerable child. God humbly revealed the Divine-self to us. Being made in the divine likeness, we are meant to imitate God. Should we then not reciprocate this epiphany? Let us reveal ourselves to God. Today could also be our epiphany when we likewise humbly

open our hearts to God. How? In prayer we open ourselves. We tell God what is in our heart of hearts, sharing our most innermost secrets."[45]

Just as God has revealed Himself to us, we are called to open ourselves up to Him. This means being honest and vulnerable in our prayers, sharing our joys and sorrows, and seeking His guidance in all aspects of our lives. This may seem daunting, but remember, everything is possible with God's grace. Through prayer and a heart filled with gratitude for His blessings, we can offer back our humility, our true selves, and our love. We offer ourselves in humble supplication as our gift to Him and our love for our neighbor.

We can pray to God as our most beloved and intimate friend. On that first epiphany, the Magi brought gold, frankincense, and myrrh gifts. Today, God would be most pleased to receive our hearts of gold to the people needing our help.

Our acts of love and compassion can take many forms. We can visit the sick, feed the hungry, provide shelter for the homeless, and offer support to those imprisoned and marginalized in our society. These are the 'frankincense' that God would be so happy to see, as they reflect His love and compassion for all His children.

Our offerings of fervent prayer are not just words, but a heartfelt conversation with our Lord and Father. We can pray for peace in the world, for the remission of sins, the salvation of souls, and the unity of all Christian people. These prayers are our 'gift of myrrh' that rise to our Lord and Father like incense, filling the heavens with our love and devotion. Like the Magi, we pay homage to God-made flesh. We know of all those things we can offer in sacrifice and are grateful for His many blessings.

Prayer: *Lord, we thank You for this epiphany You manifested to the world, to those who do not know You, and to those who consciously and unconsciously long for You. With the example shown by the Magi in offering gifts to You, may we also offer in sacrifice and in gratitude for the many blessings we have received from You, our love, and prayers for all those in need of your mercy and love, too. May we always be generous to all the people in need of help. Amen.*

CHAPTER 2

Are We True To Our Word?

(2 Corinthians 5:20 /Matthew 5:33-37)

Gospel: *"Again you have heard that it was said to your ancestors, 'Do not take a false oath, but make good to the Lord all that you vow.' But I say to you, do not swear at all; not by heaven, for it is God's throne; not by the earth, for it is his footstool; nor by Jerusalem, for it is the city of the great King. Do not swear by your head, for you cannot make a single hair white or black. Let your 'Yes' mean 'Yes,' and your 'No' mean 'No'. Anything more is from the evil one."* (Matthew 5:33-37)

In the 1st Reading, St. Paul reminds us that we are ambassadors for Christ. Do we know what that means for us? It means we have been appointed and given a high calling. We have been asked to be like diplomats of the truth. An ambassador is the primary representative or delegate of a nation or country or someone with supreme authority. He talks in front of Presidents and Kings of nations on behalf of someone with authority. St. Paul tells us that as ambassadors for Christ, we speak for Christ, act for Christ, and live for Christ. *Vive para Cristo.* To sum it up, to be like Christ. *Ser como Cristo.*

We represent Christ. Therefore, we should be a shining example for all who may listen to or see us. St. Paul even says that God exhorts us to be reconciled to God in all we do.

In the Gospel, Jesus speaks on the subject of swearing. By our human standards, this teaching seems tricky to follow because what Jesus is asking for us here is "not to swear ...." How many of us can follow this teaching? Sometimes we say, "I swear, I …. blah, blah, blah…" Are we faithful to our own word?

Is Jesus asking us not to swear at all? Of course not. We are being reminded that it is not forbidden to swear if we are swearing in truth. It is not prohibited to swear - if we are swearing in justice. It is not forbidden to swear to the honor of God or for our own truth or neighbor's just defense.

Have you been asked to be a witness or to testify in a court of law? Before you even begin to sit in testimony before a judge, you are asked to swear that "everything you say is the truth and nothing but the truth." And you invoke the help of God before you even begin.

What could be worse is when swearing becomes a habit, a standard way of speaking without considering its consequences. This can be hurtful to others, leading to a separation from God. It is a form of evil when 'the swearer' doesn't care about the harm caused by swearing falsely. This teaching serves as a reminder of the power of our words and the need to use them responsibly, in line with the teachings of Christ.

Prayer: *Good and loving God, we ask for your help and the grace that we are watchful in all that we say and do so that what we say and do is in your honor and love of neighbor. May the word of Christ dwell among us in all its richness. Glory to you Word of God, Lord Jesus Christ. Amen.*

CHAPTER 3

Who Is At The Center Of My Life?

(Matthew 16: 13-19)

Solemnity of Saints Peter and Paul

Gospel: *When Jesus went into the region of Caesaria Philippi he asked his disciples, "Who do people say that the Son of Man is?" They replied, "Some say John the Baptist, others Elijah, still others Jeremiah or one of the prophets." He said to them, "But who do you say that I am?" Simon Peter said reply, "You are the Messiah, the Son of the living God." Jesus said to him in reply, "Blessed are you, Simon son of Jonah. For flesh and blood has not revealed this to you, but my heavenly Father. And so, I say to you, you are Peter and upon this rock I will build my church and the gates of the netherworld shall not prevail against it. I will give you the keys to the kingdom of heaven. Whatever you bind on earth shall be bound in heaven; and whatever you loose on earth shall be loosed in heaven." (Matthew 16:13-19)*

Today, we commemorate the profound feast of Saints Peter and Paul, a tradition that has endured since around 250 AD. These two apostles, known for their dynamic partnership and immense influence on early Christianity, are the focus of our reflection. According to tradition, they met their martyrdom together in Rome during the persecution of Emperor Nero, with Peter crucified upside down and Paul beheaded.

Peter is the one on whom the Church is founded, the one whom Jesus called, "...*you are Peter, and upon this rock I will build my church...*" *(Matthew 16:18).* St. Paul is the apostle who had gone out to preach Jesus Christ to the Gentiles and beyond. I believe that St. Paul wrote more than any other New Testament author. One could keep talking about him because he wrote so much. The Church recognizes seven of his writings as "undisputed."[46]

In the 1st Reading, we witness Peter's unwavering faith, even in the face of imminent death while imprisoned. His steadfastness is a testament to the strength of his belief. In the 2nd Reading, St. Paul's words echo this resilience, as he assures his readers of his unwavering faith, even in the face of death, and his divine authority in teaching.

Peter and Paul, in their unwavering faith and dedication to Christ's mission, gave their lives in service to Him. Their lives were a testament to their steadfastness and commitment. They kept their gaze fixed on the face of Christ and their mission, a feat that commands our admiration and respect.

If we are to put everything and sum up both Peter's and Paul's lives, it is this: They lived their lives following a primary relationship. Jesus is the center of their lives. The meaning of their lives came from their relationship with Christ. Do we live our lives in the same way? If we don't, have we tried?

Each of them was called to follow Christ. We, too, are called to have Christ at the center of our lives. That is the very subject matter of the scripture readings today. In the Gospel, Jesus asks his disciples, *"But who do you say that I am"?(Matthew 16:15).* You can ask and try to answer the same question. It is one of the most profound theological and philosophical questions we can ask ourselves in many ways. It is not the question of "What am I?" or "What job do I have," not even the question of "What nationality do I come from," or "Where do I live"? The question "Who am I?" concerns something more profound in the core of our soul, deep into the center of our being. We see Christ. He sees us. We place Christ in the center of our lives.

Once we reflect upon the question, we will soon be led to the next question, "Who am I?". The question is about relationships. Who are the most important people and relationships in my life? What are we called to do in that relationship?

As we relate our relationship with Christ to our spouse, children, family, and friends, we recognize the importance of His presence in our lives. We pray to Jesus, who is meek and humble, to guide our interactions with compassion, kindness, and humility. With God's help, we strive to make Christ the center of our lives, a responsibility that lies within each of us.

Prayer: *As we continue and break bread together in Christ, let us thank God and also ask for the grace of having a continuing loving relationship with Him always; that we not separate from Him by our weakness; that we give God our time and worship and praying for one another and transform our faith in doing good works. May God give us the grace to continue to express that relationship with that same love for one another - today, throughout the coming week, the next, and all the days of our lives. Amen.*

CHAPTER 4

We Are Transformed By The WORD

*(1 Thessalonians 2: 9-13/**Matthew 23: 27-32**)*

Gospel: *Woe to you scribes and Pharisees, you hypocrites. You are like whitewashed tombs, which appear beautiful on the outside, but inside are full of dead men's bones and every kind of filth. Even so on the outside you appear righteous, but inside you are filled with hypocrisy and evildoing. Woe to you, scribes and Pharisees, you hypocrites. You build the tombs of the prophets and adorn the memorials of the righteous, and you say, "If we had lived in the days of our ancestors, we would not have joined them in shedding the prophets' blood. Thus you bear witness against yourselves that you are the children of those who murdered the prophets; now fill up what your ancestors measured out!" (Matthew 23:27-32)*

Are we, as individuals, faithful to ourselves? Do we truly mean what we say, or do we often find ourselves saying what we think others want to hear? When faced with indecision, do we take the time to pray and open our hearts to Jesus, our Lord and Savior? As disciples of Christ, are we intentional in our faith, or do we sometimes find ourselves doing it for the approval of others?

In the 1st Reading, St. Paul not only challenges but also encourages his fellow disciples. He reminds them, *"Working night and day in order* not to burden any of you, we proclaimed to you the gospel of God." (1 Thessalonians 2:9). He further states, "As you know, we treated each one of you as a father treats his children, exhorting and encouraging you and insisting that you conduct yourselves as worthy of the God who calls you into his kingdom and glory." (1 Thessalonians 2:11) We are not just called, but we, as responsible members of God's kingdom, are called to conduct ourselves worthily.

Jesus, in his teachings, warns the Pharisees and the scribes about the grave danger of hypocrisy – the act of appearing religious to others while minds, hearts, and souls are not aligned. It is a challenge for all of us, friends, to be vigilant and guard ourselves against this peril.

We heard some hard words, but we also had to look at them in the context of those days. We see those wordings in the Dead Sea Scrolls and Jewish-Greco-Roman writings. Therefore, we must take those words in their historical context. If we do, experts say we will understand better the meaning of scriptures and as the inspired Word of God, "not as a human concept, but as it truly is, the WORD of God." In receiving the WORD of God and in virtue of our baptism in Christ, we are transformed. We are being called to do our best to preserve the grace given to us.

Friends, our readings today challenge us to engage in a thorough examination of conscience. This is a process of self-reflection where we look inside our hearts and our whole being, seeking to understand our thoughts, words, and actions in light of our faith. We are encouraged to ask the Word to be our light for guidance prayerfully:

1. What do we desire in our hearts? Do we thank God for helping us avoid pretending and instead focus on moments of *grace?*

2. When we realize we have been given *grace,* are we turning to ourselves or our neighbor to do good? What prevents us from doing just one good thing for our neighbor today? Good things can be as simple as offering a kind word, lending a helping hand, or praying for someone in need. Let us reflect on what might be holding us back from these acts of kindness.

3. Do we forgive? Have we forgiven others? Are we loving – compassionate – caring? Forgiveness is a cornerstone of our

faith, and it is through love, compassion, and care that we reflect the teachings of Christ. Let us examine our hearts and actions in these areas, seeking to align ourselves more closely with these principles.

Prayer: *As we continue with our celebration of the Eucharist, thanking God, let us ask God for the grace to humbly challenge ourselves, to look at ourselves, and to pray to be loving, compassionate, and caring, to be forgiving, and thus to be transformed by the Word of God. May the word of Christ dwell among us in all its richness. Glory to you Word of God, Lord Jesus Christ. Amen.*

CHAPTER 5

The Greatest Love
Story Ever Told

*(Isaiah 7:10-14; **Luke 1:26-38**)*

Gospel: *In the sixth month, the angel Gabriel was sent from God to a town of Galilee called Nazareth, to a virgin betrothed to a man named Joseph, of the house of David, and the virgin's name was Mary. And coming to her, he said, "Hail favored one! The Lord is with you." But she was greatly troubled at what was said and pondered what sort of greeting this might be. Then the angel said to her, "Do not be afraid, Mary, for you have found favor with God. Behold, you will conceive in your womb and bear a son, and you shall name him Jesus. He will be great and will be called Son of the Most High, and the Lord God will give him the throne of David his father, and he will rule over the house of Jacob forever, and of his kingdom there will be no end." But Mary said to the angel, "How can this be, since I have no relations with a man?" And the angel said to her in reply, "The Holy Spirit will come upon you, and the power of the Most High will overshadow you. Therefore the child to be born will be called holy, the Son of God. And behold, Elizabeth, your relative, has also conceived a son in her old age, and this is the sixth month for her who was called barren; for nothing will be impossible for God." Mary said, "Behold, I am the handmaid of the Lord. May it be done to me according to your word." Then the angel departed from her. (Luke 1:26-38)*

This play on Broadway was on stage for many years, and in that play was this moving and memorable scene:

> "The Lord was looking over the earth, trying to decide what to do with the sinful situation on earth. The angel Gabriel approached the Lord with his horn tucked under his arm. Sensing the Lord's dilemma, Gabriel brushes his lips across the trumpet to keep the feel of it and asks, 'Lord, has the time come for me to blow the trumpet?' 'No, no,' said the Lord, 'do not touch the trumpet, not yet.'
>
> [...]Gabriel asks the Lord again what he plans to do. Will he send someone to take care of the situation? [...] Gabriel makes some suggestions, 'How about another David or Moses? You could send one of the prophets: Isaiah or Jeremiah. [...] Without looking back at Gabriel, God said, 'I am not going to send anyone to bring them the Good News. I am going to go myself.' And of course, that is what God did.'"[47]

Jesus would humble himself and live among us so that we might know His true nature. Revealing this true nature was God's way of sharing His status for our sake. God desires to be with us, to enter into a relationship with us- a relationship of love. Thus begins the most extraordinary love story ever told: the Incarnation, God made flesh, the divine love story between Creator and creature.

God chose this young woman, Mary. The angel Gabriel brought the news to Mary with great peace and joy, what we now know in our Catechism as the Annunciation to the Blessed Virgin Mary. That great moment is immortalized in the 1st Joyful Mystery of the Holy Rosary.

I would like to bring here two points the Gospel is reminding us today:

First, Mary's most significant qualification for being chosen as the mother of God was her faith in God. Mary believed when the angel told her that nothing is impossible with God. It's that simple. Do we believe in the same way that our Mother Mary believes? Despite her humble station in life, even though Mary was a virgin, she thought that God would do exactly what God said He would do. God works through people who trust in God and respond when God calls.

The Scriptures also tell us so much about many people who would respond truthfully no matter what when God calls. Jeremiah was too young and reluctant. Abraham was too old. Noah drank a lot. Moses needed more eloquence. Jonah was a complainer. David was a simple shepherd. Simon Peter had a "temper." Paul persecuted people.

There are so many of them like that, good and not so good, even bad. They are human beings like us. But they didn't know what they would experience or what would happen to their lives. But everyone experienced a life transformed by grace when they put their faith in God. God chose them because they believed. God asked them, and they responded in ways that pleased God. How do we respond when God calls us when that day and time comes? Let us remember, it is through our faith that we can experience this transformative power of God's grace.

That leads us to the second point. In this Christmas season, Mary gives us a perfect example of how to say "yes" to God. She said with utter humility and obedience, *"Behold, I am the Lord's servant. May it be done to me according to your word."(Luke 1:38).* Can we be like Mother Mary in expressing our obedience to God?

She gave her consent to whatever was in the future for her. There is no more perfect way to say "yes" to God's plan. Our "amen" to God's plan. Mary accepted and became part of God's plans. This is a love story that resonates with every person, a story that anyone who seeks to follow Jesus can relate to. It could be our love story, too, you and I, here and now. The love of God came to Mary because she trusted in God, although she did not fully understand. And because of this, she was able to follow God's will. And so can we.

Friends, God's grace will come into our lives from that great faith and trust in God. Our response to God's plan of goodness for us will carry an extraordinary connection with God. God initiates and is always the first to act in love. He will come to us if we are open to him. As we respond, we will not just enter into a love connection, but we will be enveloped in it, experiencing our most extraordinary love story with God.

The Nativity of the Lord

My sisters and brothers, through grace, we can experience a transformed life and a great and powerful love story. Remember, nothing is impossible with God. God works through us if we respond to God's call. You and I can experience power and greatness this Christmas season by saying "yes" to God's plans and purpose, like our Mother Mary.

Prayer: *As we continue with our celebration of the Eucharist, let us thank God and ask for the grace that could transform us so that we might have our very own love story – a powerful story in the world. As we anticipate God's peace and joy ourselves at Christmas, let us try to make efforts to care for one another, to see Jesus in the face of those we care for. May Christ be born in all of us so we may continue what God Himself has begun – a story of His unconditional love for us. May the word of Christ dwell among us in all its richness. May Mary, the Mother of God and our Mother too, intercede for us during this season of love and throughout the coming year. Amen.*

CHAPTER 6

Being Like A Praying Mantis

*(Acts 3: 13-15/1 John 2:1-5a/ **Luke 24: 35-48**)*

Gospel: *Then the two recounted what had taken place on the way and how he was made known to them in the breaking of the bread.*

While they were still speaking about this, he stood in their midst and said to them, "Peace be with you." But they were startled and terrified and thought that they were seeing a ghost. Then he said to them, "Why are troubled? And why do questions arise in your hearts? Look at my hands and my feet, that it is myself. Touch me and see, because a ghost does not have flesh and bones as you can see I have." And as he said this, he showed them his hands and his feet. While they were still incredulous for joy and were amazed, he asked them, "Have you anything here to eat?" They gave him a piece of baked fish; he took it and ate it in front of them.

He said to them, "These are my words that I spoke to you while I was still with you, that everything written about me in the law of Moses and in the prophets and psalms must be fulfilled." Then he opened their minds to understand the scriptures. And he said to them, "Thus, it written that the Messiah would suffer and rise from the dead on the third day, and that repentance, for the forgiveness of sins, would be preached in his name to all the nations, beginning from Jerusalem. You are witnesses of these things." (Luke 24:35-48)

Have you ever played 'hide and seek' as a kid? It's a game that can teach us a lot about our relationship with God. Just like in the game, God is always present, but sometimes we need to seek Him out. And when we do, it can be easier to find Him. And there is no more joy in that, right? That is why children play this game better, because they understand the thrill of the search and the joy of finding.

Many call "hide and seek" the poor kid's game. I happened to know that. I played that game with my siblings and friends as a kid. I was good at it by doing all sorts of disguises. In doing so, sometimes I need to remember where I was. Or to go back and find my playmates! Playing it does not cost anything, only plain fun. The wonderful thing is that, if you are creative enough, you will not be seen because you adapt to what is around you, like a *"walking stick"* or a *"praying mantis."* (These are insects that can hide even in plain sight because they absorb the colors of where they are or adapt to their immediate environment).

There are many remarkable things in our lives that we don't know about. We sometimes wish that things were not hidden even in plain sight. The best example is this: the goodness of God is all around us, but we often fail even to notice it. We don't recognize it because the good has become part of our lives. We have become too familiar with all the blessings. We know of the simple things in our lives, yet we fail to be thankful for it. Familiarity breeds ungratefulness. Things become passing fancies. We know of God's abundant goodness that is always here, yet we fail to see it. But if we cultivate a spirit of gratitude, we can start to see God's goodness in every aspect of our lives.

So, how does God respond to our human limitations? *Entonces, que hace Dios?* In His infinite wisdom and boundless love, our Father meets us where we are. *Dios desciende a nuestro propio nivel.* He descends to our level, understanding our human frailties and respecting our freedom to choose. In today's Gospel, we witness God's profound love for us as He uses our human ignorance as a tool for our growth. He does this so that the world may come to know Him and His limitless love.

God also understands that, as humans, our capacity to experience Him entirely is limited. However, this is the reason why we pray to the Holy Spirit. The Holy Spirit is our guide, our comforter, and our advocate. We hope to encounter Jesus in all the ways He has promised. He is with us daily, and we can meet Him in ways that can transform us. So, why not empower ourselves and others by performing even one act of kindness today, in Jesus' name?

Prayer: *As we continue with our celebration, let us thank God and ask for the grace to encounter Jesus even in our usual routine; to let us appear in plain sight for others while we try to bring the peace of Jesus in our hearts; that we need not hide; that instead, we should just come out of our hiding and, in humility, let people know that we care. May the word of Christ dwell among us in all its richness. Amen.*

CHAPTER 7

Proclaim It And Be
A Part Of It

*(Isaiah 49:3.5-6/ 1 Corinthians 1:1-3/ **John 1:29-34**)*

Gospel: *The next day he saw Jesus coming toward him and said, "Behold, the Lamb of God, who takes away the sin of the world. He is the one whom I said, 'A man is coming after me who ranks ahead of me because he existed before me.' I did not know him, but the reason why I came baptizing with water was that he might be known to Israel." John testified further, saying, "I saw the Spirit come down like a dove from the sky and remain upon him. I did not know him but the one who sent me to baptize with water told me, 'On whomever you see the Spirit come down and remain, he is the one who will baptize with the holy Spirit.' Now I have seen and testified that he is the Son of God." (John 1:29-34)*

Friends, today's Gospel presents a profound baptismal call. As John the Baptist beheld Jesus approaching for baptism, he proclaimed, *"Behold the Lamb of God, who takes away the sin of the world"* (John 1:29). In his distinctive preaching style, St. John sought to draw our attention to the profound significance of this Good News.

God's intention is for us to understand that kingship, friendship, and service are not separate entities, but interconnected expressions of His saving power. He invites us to share in His kingship, not as subjects, but as friends and servants, particularly to those in need. In this way, we are not just recipients of His mercy, but active participants in His divine plan.

There are two points I would like to share with you about those words: kingship, friendship, and service:

1. In a world where holiness is often overlooked, it is crucial that we seek a deeper understanding of the One whose very essence is mercy and love. We are called to tap into this understanding, to focus on the gifts that the Holy Spirit has generously bestowed upon us, fortifying us through the sacrament of baptism.

Let us not be consumed by our own problems and limitations. Like the saints in heaven, let us strive to fix our gaze on Jesus and be receptive to the *grace* of recognizing him in our life's trials. Martin Luther King, Jr., a beacon of compassion and empathy, understood the plight of the poor and oppressed. He inspired people to act peacefully, reminding us of the power of recognizing and addressing the needs of others.

We have the resources for achieving amazing things within ourselves because we will have God's *grace*. We will have God's grace if God wills it. We will have God's grace if there are no impediments and if we do not allow sin or any of our problems to overwhelm or separate us from God. We all know that achieving all these takes work. But we can try and do the best we can. One way is to reconcile ourselves with Him. Another way is to continue to discover, nurture, and use our gifts to serve Him and bring his love to others.

2. Another aspect of our baptismal call is to consider God's mercy towards all as King. This is not a passive mercy, but a mercy that calls us to action, to serve others as God serves us. It is a kingly dimension that the Lord has shared with us by our baptism, and we are challenged to put that mercy into practice by helping others.

Given this, today I want to share with you the following narrative:

"How can we tell if a person is a king or queen? They'll be wearing a crown. Thousands of years ago, people used to think that the head was an enormously powerful part of the body, because it was the part of the body closest to the sky. For this reason, kings and queens would wear crowns on their heads to show that they were extra special. [...]The king's crowns had pointed towers sticking up out of the top of them like horns. Here's a question: how can you tell if somebody is a king, if he isn't wearing a crown? By the manner they dress, or their demeanor. But kings look like the rest of us without their crowns. Again, how can you tell who's a king and who isn't? Our Bible story today tells us, that was John the Baptist's job. His job was to prepare the people for the Son of God. But how would John the Baptist know who the son of God was? [...] John the Baptist did not know. In fact, two times in the Gospel today, John said, 'I did not know him.' But as soon as John looked at Jesus, he knew that Jesus was the Messiah, the son of God. How did he know? Jesus did have the Holy Spirit in Him. [...]That's a whole lot better than a crown, isn't it? The One, (God) who sent him to baptize gave John insight, so that he could say 'Now I have seen for myself.'"[48]

This quote is long, but every line is meaningful. We are grateful to the author and source for such profound insights. The narrative tells us clearly how John the Baptist, a significant figure in our faith, might have known Jesus by himself, through Jesus himself. John, who was chosen by God to prepare the way for Jesus, may not have known without the *grace* of knowing from God Himself.

It also tells us how we ought to learn and understand the meaning of our Lord's ministry for our lives. All of us are called to tell the story of the Baptist's encounter with Jesus. We have our own stories, too. Stories of blessings and graces received ever since we were baptized, a sacrament that symbolizes our initiation into the Christian faith, may help transform ourselves and the world.

Through parables and stories from the Bible, we are called to proclaim the redemptive message of the immense love and mercy demonstrated by Jesus. His life, from birth to resurrection, offers a roadmap for personal transformation and societal betterment. Importantly, we are not mere spectators, but active participants in this incredible narrative.

Prayer: *My Lord and God, You are my hope and strength. Without You, I fall into sin. Help me to follow Jesus faithfully and to live according to his will. May the word of Christ dwell in me in all its richness. Make me holy in mind and heart, and always eager to serve You with all the love of my heart. Thank You for your grace in seeing me as I am, continually renewing the life of grace that You gave me in baptism. Help me always to grow in Your love, contemplate Your glory and Spirit everywhere, and thank You for Your boundless mercy. Amen.*

CHAPTER 8

God's Grace In Two Vocation Stories

Nicodemus
(John 3:1-7)

Gospel: *Now there was a Pharisee named Nicodemus, a ruler of the Jews. He came to Jesus at night and said to him, "Rabbi, we know that you are a teacher who has come from God, for no one can do these signs that you are doing, unless God is with him." Jesus answered and said to him, "Amen, amen, I say to you, no one can see the kingdom of God without being born from above. " Nicodemus said to him, "How can a person once grown old be born again? Surely he cannot reenter his mother's womb and be born again can he?" Jesus answered, "Amen, amen, I say to you, no one can enter the kingdom of God without being born of water and Spirit. What is born of flesh is flesh and what is born of spirit is spirit. Do not be amazed that I told you, 'You must be born from above.'" (John 3:1-7)*

Nicodemos was a puzzled man. We know from the accounts that he was a man with many honors. A highly respected leader. The Jews considered him a great teacher of the Law. And yet, something was lacking in his life. So he came to Jesus for a talk so that somehow, in the darkness of night, he might find light. He told Jesus that people were impressed with the signs that Jesus did. Jesus said to him that to see the Kingdom of God; one needs to be "born from above" (the Greek word is *anothen,* which also means *"born again"*).

Jesus and Nicodemus

In Jesus' answer, we see that the important thing was not the signs; the important thing was the change in a man's inner life, which could only be described as a new birth. This 'new birth' is a metaphorical term used to describe a profound spiritual transformation, a complete change in one's perspective, values, and priorities. There was more to the answer that Nicodemus received. In his heart, there was a tremendous unsatisfied longing, an infinite yearning, yet in his own life experience, such yearning was impossible to achieve. That was the underlying reason why he wanted to see Jesus.

Nicodemus is up against the eternal problem, the problem of the man who wants to be changed and cannot change himself. To be born anew is to undergo a radical change, like a new birth; it is to have something that affects the soul, which can only be akin to being born all over again; and the entire process is not a human achievement because it comes from the grace and power of God. That's what Baptism brings. Baptism brings the power of God and infuses that grace, the grace that enables us to share in His divine life. That, my friend, is called divine grace, *sanctifying grace.* Jesus does not miss a teachable moment.

Jonah
(Jonah 2:1-11)

Scripture: *This is the word of the LORD that came to Jonah, son of Amittai: "Set out for the great city of Nineveh, and preach against it; their wickedness has come up before me." But Jonah made ready to flee to Tarshish away from the LORD. He went down to Joppa, found a ship going to Tarshish, paid the fare, and went aboard to journey with them to Tarshish, away from the LORD.*

The LORD, however, hurled a violent wind upon the sea, and in the furious tempest that arose the ship was on the point of breaking up. Then the mariners became frightened and each one cried to his god. To lighten the ship for themselves, they threw its cargo into the sea. Meanwhile, Jonas had come down into the hold of the ship, and lay there fast asleep. The captain came to him and said, "What are you doing asleep? Rise up, call upon your God! Perhaps God will be mindful of us so that we may not perish."

Then they said to one another, "Come, let us cast lots to find out on whose account we have met with this misfortune." So they cast lots, and thus singled out Jonah. "Tell us," they said, "what is your business? Where do you come from? What is your country, and to what people do you belong?" "I am a Hebrew," Jonah answered them; "I worship the LORD, the God of heaven, who made the sea and the dry land.

Now the men were seized with great fear and said to him, "How could you do such a thing?" – They knew that he was fleeing from the LORD, because he had told them. – "What shall we do with you," they asked, "that the sea may quiet down for us?" For the sea was going more and more turbulent. (Jonah 2:1-11)

Unlike Nicodemus, Jonah allowed himself to be subjected to embarrassment. He was even ridiculed. The Prophet Jonah stayed in the belly of the great fish for three days and three nights, and while he was in the belly, according to the Bible story, he prayed a psalm of thanksgiving to the Lord. After he prayed, the Lord commanded the fish to spew him upon the shore. The fish obeyed, for the fish is just fish. Jonah was not hurt, of course, when he landed on the sea shore. If he was, that could have been another embarrassment.

I read the Book of Jonah a long time ago, and mind you, it was only two pages long. I will reread it and I suggest that you re-read it too. Even as a kid, I loved the story not only because of its humorous nature, instructive aspect, and the sublime lesson that can be learned but also because it offers a graphical image of how God loves and plays with his children. God "swooping" us up on our way to heaven, just like when God made the great fish let go of Jonah after three days and three nights in the darkness of its belly. Being in the dark and then seeing the light reminds us of the sign of our continuing journey to God through dying and being raised, a gift of God's love for us despite our sins!

The people of Nineveh repented at the preaching of Jonah (*Matthew 12:40-41*). The book of Jonah paves the way for the gospel, with its message of redemption for all of us. The story is a stark reminder of God's threatened punishments for the disobedient, but more importantly, it is a testament to the love and mercy of our Father, which compels us all to repent and seek forgiveness. It is a story that humbles us and fills us with gratitude for the forgiveness we receive through God's mercy, especially in the sacrament of Baptism.

In the Christian faith, Baptism is a symbol of forgiveness. It represents the merciful will and love of our God for us. Through Baptism, we are united with Christ, becoming one with Him. When God forgives our sins, they are washed away in the blood of the Lamb, leaving us as pure as snow. This act of forgiveness is akin to being 'born again,' a concept that Nicodemus struggled to comprehend. This is why he posed the question that sparked a deeper understanding of our faith.

So, there we are. Two vocation stories. One a reminder that we must not stay in the gray realm of doubt but to live in the radiant light of God's love, ready to answer any questions we might have for our salvation. The other is another reminder of the Father's mercy and forgiveness for our transgressions.

Why do I call them vocation stories? As deacons, we teach, preach, and practice what we preach. To the best of our God-given abilities, we follow the ordaining Bishop's exhortation to us. *A herald of the Gospel you have become. Believe what you read, teach what you believe, practice what you teach.* In the story about Jonah, we can find these three essential elements of a vocation: teaching, preaching, and practicing what we preach. Even after being ordained, I am still on that long and challenging journey, responding to the calling that God began in me in Baptism. These stories also constitute the very pattern of how anyone, in the encounter with the Holy Spirit through Baptism, may become a faithful Christian.

For in Baptism, we encounter Jesus as we unite with him. As we join him, we want to become even more of a true disciple. When we are baptized into Him, all the hope and energy that fuels our lives are derived from this moment of encounter, when the freedom of the gracious God visits the dark areas of our lives to "swoop us up" to the place prepared for us, life eternal.

In Baptism, we were given the gift of becoming like him. Therefore, we pray for the grace to always remember those gifts given in sacrificial love and respond to that love as He draws us into Him. We only have to open ourselves, seek and discover, nurture, and cherish those gifts with all our hearts, minds, and strength.

When we can do that through God's gift of grace, we will know that the Lord puts words of wisdom into our mouths. Those words are teachable moments that are only possible through the action of the Holy Spirit. This passage in Proverbs reminds us of this: "Lo! *I will pour out to you my spirit; I will acquaint you with my words.*" (Proverbs 1:23). This reminder must always be our guiding principle that the Holy Spirit is present in us and will help us to express the words of truth that God puts into our mouth.

Prayer: *Almighty Father, Divine Teacher, may you give us your grace to recognize teachable moments in our lives. O Holy Spirit, enkindle in us the fire of your love. Move us to repent of our sins. Lord Jesus, the Father's only begotten Son, teach us to be like You. Unite us with You so that we may become your faithful disciples. Amen.*

CHAPTER 9

Seeing With The Heart Of Jesus

(1 Samuel 16:1b, 6-7, 10-13a/
*Ephesians 5:8-14 / **John 9:1-41**)*

Gospel: *As he passed by he saw a man blind from birth. His disciples asked him. "Rabbi, who sinned, this man or his parents, that he was born blind.?" Jesus answered, "Neither he nor his parents sinned; it is so that the works of God might be made visible through him. We have to do the works of the one who sent me while it is day. Night is coming when no one can work. While I am in the world, I am the light of the world." When he had said this, he spat on the ground and made clay with the saliva, and smeared the clay on his eyes, and said to him, "Go wash in the Pool of Siloam" (which means Sent). So he went and washed, and came back able to see.*

His neighbors and those who had seen him earlier as a beggar said, "Isn't this the one who use to sit and beg?" Some said, "It is," but others said, "No, he just looks like him." He said, "I am." So they said to him, "[So] how were your eyes opened?" He replied, "The man called Jesus made clay and anointed my eyes and told me, 'Go to Siloam and wash.' So I went there and washed and was able to see." And they said to him, "Where is he?" He said, "I don't know."

They brought the one who has once blind to the Pharisees. Now Jesus had made clay and opened his eyes on a sabbath. So

– 139 –

then the Pharisees also asked him how he was able to see. He said to them, "He put clay on my eyes, and I washed, and now I can see." So some of the Pharisees said, "This man is not from God, because he does keep the sabbath." [But] others said, "How can a sinful man do such signs?" And there was a division among them. So they said to the blind man again, "What do you have to say about him, since he opened your eyes?" He said, "He is a prophet."

Now the Jews did not believe that he had been blind and gained his sight until they summoned the parents of the one who had gained his sight. They asked them, "Is this your son, who say was born blind? How does he now see?" His parents answered and said, "We know that this is our son and that he was born blind. We do not know how he sees now, now do we know who opened his eyes. Ask him, he is of age; he can speak for himself." His parents said this because they were afraid of the Jews, for the Jews had already agreed that if anyone acknowledges him as the Messiah, he would be expelled from the synagogue. For this reason his parents said, "He is of age, question him."

So a second time they called the man who had been born blind and said to him, "Give God the praise! We know that this man is a sinner." He replied, "If he is a sinner, I do not know. One thing I do know is that I was blind and now I see." So they said to him, "What did he do to you? How did he opened your eyes?" He said to them, "I told you already and you did not listen. Why do you want to hear it again? Do you want to become his disciples too?" They ridiculed him and said, "You are that man's disciple; we are disciples of Moses! We know that God spoke to Moses, but we do not know where this one is from."

The man answered and said to them, "This is what is so amazing, that you do not know where he is from, yet he opened my eyes. We know that God does not listen to sinners, but if one is devout and does his will, he listens to him. It is unheard of that anyone opened the eyes of a person born blind. If this man were not from God he would not be able to do anything." They answered and said to him, "You were born totally in sin, and are you trying to teach us?" Then they threw him out.

When Jesus heard that they had thrown him out, he found him and said, "Do you believe in the Son of Man?" He answered and said, "Who is he, sir, that I may believe in him?" Jesus said to him, "You have seen him and the one speaking with you is he." He said, "I do believe, Lord," and he worshipped him. Then Jesus said, "I came into this world for judgment, so that those who do not see might see, and those who do see might become blind."

Some of the Pharisees who were with him heard this and said to him, "Surely we are not also blind, are we?" Jesus said to them, "If you were blind, you would have no sin; but now you are saying, 'We see,' so your sin remains." (John 9: 1-41)

(Close your eyes)...If you close your eyes, what do you see? Nothing. We are blind. Then, if you rub your eyes *(touch one eye slowly)*, you begin to see. It feels different.

But what if we keep our eyes closed? Something remains if we remain silent, still, calm, and focused long enough, blocking everything we can think of from the outside world. Our heartbeat. Right? We can feel it. We can hear it.

It is a profound dichotomy. We are endowed with physical eyes to perceive the world. Yet, Jesus beckons us to transcend this limited vision and see with our hearts rich with compassion. He has blessed us with a heart capable of love and compassion, a spiritual sight that can illuminate the darkest corners of our existence.

Our encounter with Jesus through the Gospel today is truly remarkable. Jesus sees people for who they are. He loves them. God forgives them. When Jesus saw this man blind from birth, he didn't just pass by. He did something extraordinary, something that might seem strange to us today. He made a mud paste using his own spit and applied it to the blind man's eyes. Then, he instructed the man to wash in the pool of Siloam. Can you imagine witnessing such a scene? It's a testament to the power and compassion of our Lord.

How many times have we asked the Lord to pass by, like this blind man, so that He can heal us from our blindness, sickness, and afflictions? How do we show our gratitude to Him? Do we love Him in return? Do we try to help those physically and spiritually blind in the spirit that Jesus did? Can we see and feel with our hearts as Jesus did?

The Pharisees, the religious leaders of Jesus' day, didn't believe Jesus healed the man. Of course, it was unheard of for anyone to open the eyes of a man born blind, just using mud paste, until the coming of Christ. Not only that, but they were also angry with Jesus because Jesus healed him on a Sabbath Day. They could not see Jesus with their heart. They were spiritually blind.

In the Gospel today, the man born blind experiences a profound transformation. He receives both physical and spiritual light from Christ. His eyes were opened to the healing heart of Christ. He saw the light. Similarly, in the 2nd Reading, Paul invites his community to live up to their status as children of God by living as children of light, *"producing every kind of goodness and righteousness and truth."* *(Ephesians 5:9-10).* We were once in darkness, but now we *"are light in the Lord" (Ephesians 5:8).* This is a powerful message of hope and renewal. Let us reflect on it and strive to show our families and friends that we are children of the light.

Let us respond to the Gospel like the newly healed, blind man: by worshipping, praying, and doing the good works of the Gospel—like our Baptisms call us to be. Today, let us respond by praying for the Elect in our parish, in all parishes, and those preparing for baptism. Through the Gospel, we are all given opportunities to reflect deeply on our imperfections and show kindness and justice to everyone. This is not a passive call, but an active one. We are empowered to make a difference in the world around us.

To live as children of God. Let this week be the week that Jesus anoints our eyes so we can see clearly. Through prayer, let us ask Jesus to send us to our personal pools of Siloam to wash and see the truth of Christ.

Prayer: *Lord Jesus, fill my heart with faith and love. Look with love upon me, the love You showed me when You delivered yourself to unbelieving and evil men and suffered the agony of the cross. Fill my mind, heart, and soul with the light of your Gospel. Teach me to follow your example and create a new spirit in me. I ask for perseverance in faith, especially during these weeks of Lent. I pray for your grace to be able to pray more often so that I may see you pass by to cure my sinfulness and spiritual blindness. Deepen my vision. Then I, too, can open my eyes to see Your Light. Let it guide me to live a life of holiness and allow me to see myself and others through Your eyes. Amen.*

CHAPTER 10

You Are More Than Just A Number!

*(Acts 13:14, 43-52/ Revelations 7:9, 14b-17/**John 10: 27-30**)*

Gospel: *My sheep hear my voice; I know them, and they follow me. I give them eternal life and they shall not perish. No one can take them out of my hand. My Father, who has given them to me, is greater than all, and no one can take them out of the Father's hand. The Father and I are one." (John 10:27-30)*

When Jesus says, *"My sheep hear my voice; I know them, and they follow me" (John 10:27)*, we feel an immediate connection with Him. This connection is not just a fleeting moment, but a deep-rooted assurance of His love and care. When Jesus says, *"...no one can take them out of my hand" (John 10:28)*, there is a profound sense of belonging and closeness to our Savior, a reassurance that we are safe and secure in His embrace.

Words are moving and dynamic. They carry us, too. John's Gospel is like that. It speaks of intimacy—an encounter. St. John's words echo a promise and a response. We desire to hold on to Jesus's hands so tight we don't want to let go, like two lovers who intimately know each other and what love really is. We already know that Jesus loves us. Our response then is not just to love Him more, but to devote ourselves to Him, to reciprocate His love with our own.

The Good Shepherd wants us to know that he cares for and loves us with an everlasting love that calls us by name. He knows all our names. He knows each member of his flock. We are not just one sheep in the flock. We are not just a number. We are more than just a number! Each of us holds a unique and significant place in His heart, and that is something to be cherished and valued.

No one can snatch us away from the Father's hand. We need that reminder, for there are all kinds of things in life that can threaten us. But despite the senseless hurts we see in the world today, the danger and death that are part of our lives, we also know that God is greater than any danger. Our second Reading reminds us that "...*God will wipe away every tear from their eyes*" *(Revelations 7:17)*. When we are hurting, God eases the pain that causes us to cry.

That's the Good News of salvation. Whatever happens *to us* is not as important as what's in us. Hearing the voice of Jesus means God is *in us*. In believing, we may have life in his name. Believing is following. That's the essence of Christian life: to become attuned to the voice of the Good Shepherd resonating in our hearts to follow Him and not be lost.

As Jesus sends his love and devotion for us, how do we assert that same devotion and love for him and his flock in return? By remembering our baptismal promises. Through intimation with the Lord in prayer. Through caring for his sheep. Through our voices, we comfort those entrusted to our care. Like the Good Shepherd, to go after the stray sheep. To be joyful in bringing them back.

God knows us. *"I give them eternal life, and they shall never perish. No one can take them out of my hand." (John 10:28).* That's a promise that God made us from the beginning of time. That's why Jesus founded the Church. To bring us all to eternal salvation. Easter's mystery reminds us that eternal salvation is available to all. If we want to belong to Jesus, we must hear his voice. We need to stay connected with him. So that we will not stray away from him; remember, we are more than just a number.

Prayer: *As we break bread together, let us thank God and implore the Spirit to give us the grace to help us recognize Christ's voice in our hearts and be thankful for that grace. May the word of Christ dwell among us in all its richness. If we have a significant decision to make today, tomorrow, or in the future, let us pray and listen to what our Good Shepherd suggests. Amen.*

CHAPTER 11

Another Friend!

(John 14:15-21)

Gospel: "*If you love me, you will keep my commandments. And I will ask the Father, and he will give you another Advocate to be with you always, the Spirit of truth, which the world cannot accept, because it neither sees nor knows it. But you know it, because it remains with you, and will be in you. I will not leave you orphans; I will come to you. In a little while the world will no longer see me, but you will see me, because I live and you will live. On that day you will realize that I am in my Father and you are in me and I in you. Whoever has my commandments and observes them is the one who loves me. And whoever loves me will be loved by my Father, and I will love him and reveal myself to him.*" (John 14:15-21)

Today, our lesson from John's Gospel is noticeably clear and powerful. Let's recall the Last Supper, a significant event in the life of Jesus and his disciples. They broke bread and shared from the cup, symbolizing the body and blood of Jesus. Jesus, in a profound act of humility, washed the disciples' feet, demonstrating the importance of service and love. Judas, one of the disciples, has just left them and went over the fence, setting in motion the events that would lead to Jesus' crucifixion. He disappeared somewhere, leaving a void in the group.

Here, Jesus is telling the disciples that he will be leaving them. Jesus is preparing the disciples for his absence. He says: *"And I will ask the Father, and he will give you another Advocate to be with you always, the Spirit of truth which the world cannot accept, because it neither sees nor knows it .But you know it, because it remains with you and will be in you. I will not leave you orphans; I will come to you."(John 14:16-18.).* But he did not only prepare the disciples for his absence, but our Lord also had all of us in mind. He also prepared us with His Spirit remaining in us. Not only that, but God also sent us a friend like no other—the Holy Spirit, a divine presence that is beyond human comprehension.

In Greek, the word for "another Advocate" is *"allon parakleton."* This term is significant as it emphasizes the unique role of the Holy Spirit as a comforter, helper, and advocate for the disciples and believers.[49] The phrase means "one who is called alongside to help." You and I, not being Greek, can take that translation. It is close enough. Here is this story I picked for this particular day, which I hope may give more light to this translation:

> "An old man and his wife are sitting in the parking lot of a shopping mall. The hood is up on their car. [...] A stranger approached the old gentleman. [...]The stranger looks under the hood, but then, he is no more knowledgeable about automobile engines than the old man. He assures the old man he will return,[50] and then he drove to a nearby service station. There, he explains the situation to the mechanic and says he will pay him if he would help the elderly couple with their car.
>
> Returning with the mechanic, the stranger gets into a conversation with the old gentleman. The stranger is wearing a ring, signifying that he had been a Marine. Coincidentally, so had the old man. He confides that he had served in some of the harshest battles in our nation's history, including Guadalcanal and Okinawa. He had retired from the Marine Corps after the war.

After the car was repaired and running, the old gentleman handed a card to the stranger, and they shook hands and parted. Later, the stranger happened to look at the card. The name of the old gentlemen was on the card in a golden leaf and under his name was written: Congressional Medal of Honor Society. It was only then that the former Marine realized that he had come to the aid of one of America's heroes.

Just a reminder this Memorial Day weekend, that there are people who had served their country [...] It is only right that we recognize their sacrifice and honor their memory this holiday weekend."[51]

But there is also another translation of that Greek phrase—'another friend,' which I find particularly comforting. 'Another Friend.' With the capital letters. This phrase resonates deeply, especially when we find ourselves in unexpected situations, like the elderly couple who needed someone to come alongside them. It's a reminder that we all could be in that situation sooner or later—the need for Another Friend.

At times, we find ourselves in need, and someone comes alongside us. That is the work of the Holy Spirit. But the Holy Spirit is not just a guide, He is also a friend, a counselor, a comforter. And sometimes, without us even realizing, the Holy Spirit serves in these capacities, providing us with the support and guidance we need.

The Gospel reminds us of a profound truth-the same Spirit that was in Christ is the Spirit that will be with us in our time of need. Christ departed from this world so that His Spirit could be available to every person who opens themselves to Him. Reflect on this for a moment: 'And *I will ask the Father, and he will give you another Advocate to be with you always...*'

In other words, God comes alongside us, as the Greek phrase 'Allon Parakleton' suggests, in times of hurt or need. He is our Comforter, Counselor, Advocate, Companion, and Friend.

May you all have a fun week. Happy Memorial Day to you all.

Prayer: *Heavenly Father, You glorified our Lord Jesus and sent us Your Spirit. You have opened the way to eternal life. You have shared these gifts and increased my love of God. You made my faith more robust and stronger day by day. Thank You for sending me your Spirit to cleanse my life and to share with me through the Eucharist, You, as my Bread of Life. Amen.*

CHAPTER 12

A Mother Like No Other

(John 15:9-17)

Mother's Day

Gospel: *As the Father loves me, so I love you. Remain in my love. If you keep my commandments, you will remain in my love, just as I kept my Father's commandments and remain in his love. I have told you this, so that my joy might be in you and your joy might be complete. This is my commandment: love one another as I love you. No one has greater love than this, to lay down one's life for one's friends. You are my friends if you do what I command you. I no longer call you slaves, because a slave does not know what his master is doing. I have called you friends, because I have told you everything I have heard from my Father. It was not you who chose me, but I who chose you and appointed you to go and bear fruit that will remain, so that whatever you ask the Father in my name he may give you. This I command you: love one another. (John 15:9-17)*

Good morning, and Happy Mother's Day to all mothers and mother figures in our fellowship of faith. On this particular day, we would like to thank all of you, dear mothers, who shape our lives and serve as our safe place as we go out into the world. Mothers have a unique power to influence their children no matter what. Like this story, I would like to share with you:

"The former police chief of Knoxville, Tennessee, Phil Keith was in a televised press conference. [...] he received a call from his mother while he was talking. Phil knew his mother would not call him under those circumstances unless something was seriously wrong, so he excused himself [...] to answer the phone.

When his mother picked up the phone, she said: 'Phil Keith, are you chewing gum'? He said. 'Um, yes ma'am.'

She said, 'Well, it looks awful. Spit it out.'

So, [...] Phil Keith spit out his gum and returned to finish the press conference. Isn't it amazing the power mothers have in our lives?'"[52]

It's not easy being a mom. Even when your kids have grown up, it is somewhat difficult to stay away from them. Those of you who have children know that regardless of their age. For example, a mom in this story was beginning to find this the hard way:

"This Mom says that she is going to try something different this summer with their dog and their kids. She's sending the dog to camp, and she's sending the kids to obedience school. [...] Writer Erma Bombeck once said; 'What mother has never fallen on her knees when she has gone into her son's bedroom and prayed, 'Please God, no more. You were only supposed to give me what I could handle.'"[53]

It's not easy being a mother. You can't just shake your kids off away from your lives. They keep coming back. Especially when you don't need them. On the other side, it's not easy having a mom either. Kids just can't shake you off too, right?

"There is that saying that runs like this: 'The hand that rocks the cradle usually is attached to someone who is not getting enough sleep.'[...] The comedian George Wallace said: 'I grew up hearing stupid things. Mother would say, 'that's the last time I'm going to tell you to take out the garbage. Well, George says, 'thank God.'"[54]

Mothers often say their kids do not listen to them anymore. How many times have we heard that from mother? It is even more challenging when they become adults.

Deeply loving mothers never left our side. They taught us to be winners in life. How fortunate are we to be their child. Our mother's smiles, attitudes, and outlook in life brightened our days. Our mothers have been our inspirations and allowed us to forget our problems and miseries. They always told us to try to be successful in life. Try saying yes, Mother! Or, say yes and mean it. They are not even asking too much. They know no one doesn't get to become successful quickly. That's why we love moms!

Think back to the countless loving sacrifices your mother made for you. As they age, you witness their struggles and it breaks your heart. Often, our mothers didn't need to say much, just a simple 'I love you.' Sometimes, they didn't even say that. But their love was evident in the sacrifices they made, day in and day out. I am grateful every day for the love and care my mother showed upon me.

I don't know about you, but I do not want to forget how grateful I am to God for the rest of my life because I have a mother. One is my mother, who is now in the company of the angels in Heaven, and the other mother I have is a mother like no other, the Mother of God.

Let us show our appreciation for them all: mothers, grandmothers, great-grandmothers, and those who are like mothers to us.

Let us express our gratitude by giving them material and spiritual things, loving them more, and praying to our Blessed Mother for their benefit more often.

The Child Jesus and Mother Mary

Today's Gospel is perfect for Mother's Day because it is about love. In His *grace*, our ever-loving God reminded us with a call and a command. Remember when an expert tested Jesus in the Law by asking him: "Teacher, which commandment in the law is the greatest?" Jesus replied: *"You shall love the Lord, your God, with all your heart, with all your soul, and with all your mind. This is the greatest and the first commandment. The second is like it: You shall love your neighbor as yourself. The whole Law and the prophets depend on these two commandments." (Matthew 22:37-40).* It's all about love—the one true love with the Father. And as members of this community, it is our role and privilege to spread this love, to embody these commandments in our daily lives.

God acts out of love to reinforce our understanding or correct our misinterpretations. We repeatedly see this call to love in the many pages of the scriptures. And yet, we sometimes fail to express them when it is needed. Even in our families, we find it difficult to express our love or to speak so lovingly about our love. I remember a time when I held back from saying 'I Love You' to a family member, only to regret it later. It was a lesson that taught me the importance of expressing love when we feel it, not waiting until it's too late. Today, we can focus on what Jesus says about the greatest commandment.

Why would Jesus be so focused on love? Because early in life, as a child, he learned the power of love from Mary and Joseph! He knew the love of neighbors and friends and discovered that love has a transformative power. Love heals not just the body, but also the heart, mind, and spirit. It has the power to heal you and me, bringing hope and renewal.

Prayer: *Let us thank God, and as we continue with our celebration of the Holy Eucharist, let us ask the Lord for the grace to help us put into practice what the Lord has commanded us to do: love others as we love ourselves, do what Mother Mary has asked us, do whatever He tells us to do, be God's friends, be our Mother Mary's friends, too, and love each other as we have been loved. Amen.*

CHAPTER 13

Our Destiny With God

On Jesus Falling a Total Of Three Times While Carrying The Cross
(a reflection on the 3rd, 7th, and 9th Stations Of The Cross – delivered
at St. Catherine of Alexandria Church, Morgan Hill, CA)

*"A voice I did not know said to me: 'I freed your shoulder
from the burden; your hands were freed from the
load. You called, in distress, and I saved you."*
– Psalm 81:7-8

Not only was Jesus sentenced to die on the cross, subjected to unbearable beatings and humiliation, but he was to carry the cross the soldiers would later use to kill him through the narrow, crowded streets of Jerusalem. You can imagine the city was full of people, many of whom mocked and took pleasure in watching as our Lord struggled to carry the cross over his shoulders.

Stretched to breaking point, with the weight of the wood and the pain on his back, after the horrendous physical punishment inflicted on him, Jesus becomes so exhausted and falls *a total of three (3) times*.

Friends, there are three points I would like to make in this reflection:

1. It was not falling once, twice, or three times that was most significant; instead, he got up as many times. Jesus stood up repeatedly to continue his agonizing journey in fulfilling his destiny.

Under much less weight, we fall every day, too. We are only sometimes on our way to a life-changing event. We are not always looking up to an encounter with God. Too often, we fail because we stray from the path that God has set before us. We succumb to unforgiveness. We fall due to our sins.

We need to recover from our sins and carry on, just as Jesus repeatedly got back on his feet.

We must keep our hearts and minds focused on God when we feel powerless, vulnerable, confused, and struggle to make life-changing decisions.

Forty-six years ago, I found myself agonizing about deciding to come to America. My parents during that time were in their 70s, suffering from life-threatening illnesses. My mom has cancer. My dad was suffering from many severe diseases, so he could no longer take care of himself. I was confused.

My U.S. visa was soon to expire. I prayed so hard to the Lord for guidance. I struggled between leaving my parents in that state or condition and going to America so that I could provide a better future for my young family. I choose the latter.

I was in tears when I left my family, my beautiful wife, and my two wonderful children and landed in the Bay Area. Two months later, my father died. I was not able to come home at the burial of my father. Alone in America, away from my loved ones, the sadness, emptiness, and loneliness were almost unbearable.

Being new in this "land of opportunity" amidst the cultural shock, the transition toward a different norm of life was not easy. My attention turned to the Child Jesus, who, as an exile, with help from his parents, escaped from "the land of the Herods." I became more dependent on our Mother Mary and Saint Joseph, the Holy Family of Jesus, asking for their intercession and help.

Thinking about my mother, who was fighting to stay alive from cancer, my prayers to our Lady got me through those days and continue even during these present, challenging times.

I prayed to my Guardian Angel for his guidance and protection every day. The light will come when you try to be more attentive to God's voice.

Before I knew it, I was up and walking again, resuming my life's journey.

Friends, when we feel sad, empty, and confused, we must be attentive to God's voice. This voice, often found in scripture, prayer, or the wise counsel of others, can guide us to resume our life journey with assurance and hope. For instance, it might remind us of a time when we overcame a similar struggle, or it might offer a new perspective on our situation.

We need the Holy Spirit in our daily lives. We need to find the inner strength to rise again from our cross.

We have sometimes doubted our ability or felt people may be doubting us. We have had times when we thought we were not successful at work or that, as a community, things were at a standstill. We have had times when we got tired and didn't want to continue. These struggles are not signs of weakness or lack of faith, but rather, they are normal parts of our journey. They are opportunities for us to lean on God and each other, and to grow in our faith.

But take heart, for Jesus truly understands. He comprehends our weariness and our falls, for he, too, experienced them. As the weight of the cross grows heavier, and the concerns for our loved ones intensify, the struggle to rise becomes more daunting. Yet, in these moments, we can find solace in the fact that Jesus has been there, too.

We continue to try our best until we are up and walking again. But we don't have to be heroes. Jesus shows us that being heroic does not mean staying on one's feet at all costs. It means each of us, gets up again after falling and starting on our chosen path.

Human beings, like Jesus, are resilient. They rise again, shoulder their burdens, confront challenges, and strive for a 'promised land of complete liberation.'

Amid our search for hope, we come to another point:

2. We don't give up.

Some face setbacks in our financial, health, and political systems, but we don't give up. We persist.

Some fear the prospect of unemployment for themselves, through no fault of their own, but because of the pandemic or the economy. Some have lost their jobs. They feel that they have little hope of finding employment. But we don't give up.

Some suffer from isolation and loneliness or are surprised by a cancer diagnosis or a life-threatening illness, and it seems this is the end for them. But we don't give up.

Fourteen years ago, I was diagnosed with cancer. I had been subjected to many trials and carried my cross each time despite the heavy weight of the cross on my shoulders, but this one was different. This impending fall from the cross seemed permanent. I was devastated. I thought that was the end for me. I asked the Lord to spare me from it.

Cancer is a dreadful disease. A couple of my close friends died from it. My mom died from it. My brother-in-law died from it. My cousin died from it. But, I prayed to our Lord, our Mother Mary, and the Saints that that too, for me, might come to pass. And it did. My surgery was successful. No complications. I was grateful to my doctors and for family and friends who all prayed for me. Praise God for that. Now, I am cancer-free. As it turned out, God had other plans for me. And here I am.

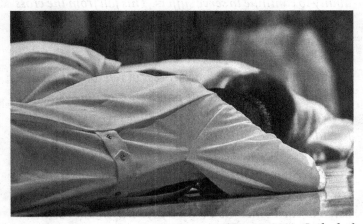

My ordination as a Permanent Deacon, May 12, 2012, Cathedral Basilica of San Jose, California (Photo by: Sonja May)

As I lay down at the foot of God's altar, I realized I am nothing but whole and at peace in the Lord. I prayed to rise from there as a deacon forever.

People are burdened by the crosses of hardships they carry all around them. We struggle and sometimes fall, but we don't give up.

Many today feel that they are at that moment of final falling. Crushed by the weight of their crosses, they cannot get up or go on. Some stay down. Some go on. As they continue, their lives change for the better, and they become much better. They didn't give up.

We are a lot stronger than we think we are. Yes, we are nervous because we already somewhat know the outcome—or not. But yes, we are fearful because of the many unknowns in our lives. Or because we know what has happened to other people. What other people experienced had an effect on their lives that seemed to keep them down.

But Jesus is with each one of us, no matter how we fall. He chooses to love and save us there. This image of Jesus in our reflection today should carry us through.

> *Two years ago, my wife suffered a major stroke that left the right side of her body paralyzed. She uses a wheelchair even to this day and needs a lot of help as she is unable to function as normally as before. As her sole caregiver, when she suffers, I also suffer. Our children suffer. Our ability to continue to serve suffers. This fall from the cross of our lives has changed our way of life; I believe we look at life and how we live it differently now.*

> *While she is still in the long process of rehabilitation and treatment, we don't take life passively anymore. Since we retired from gainful employment, time has become a dear friend. We take our time when we eat, and we enjoy our food more. We joked, smiled, and laughed with each other more. We have gained new friends. Our relationship with friends and family has taken us to a new level. We try to listen to each other more. We try to cherish our moments together. We try to listen to our kids more. We try to be more attentive to God's voice.*

> *We give thanks to God every time we feel His presence, whenever we receive His grace, and for the many blessings we have received.*

These words from St. Paul's 1st Letter to the Thessalonians and for us serves as a reminder: *"pray unceasingly...In all circumstances give thanks, for this is the will of God for you, in Christ Jesus."* (1 Thessalonians

5:16-17). Prayer is our refuge when thrown into oblivion. Giving thanks to God elevates our spirit toward Him.

And now, I come to my third and final point:

3.   Staying focused on our destiny.

In Jesus, we find hope and encouragement. We put our unbounded trust. Jesus is our strength.

Jesus' falling three times reminds us that even in our moments of complete helplessness, in our experiences of depression, in walking through the desert of our lives, in falling from the weight of our cross, on our way to our own Calvary, we can stand up again.

We focus on our destiny. What is our destiny? Eternal life with God.

How do we focus on our destiny?

Remember the things that happened in your life or your life with others: your loved ones, your children, your friends, your parents, your brothers and sisters, your community.

In trying to go back to those moments, this reminder from the Book of Psalms comes to us as it is written: *"A voice I did not know said to me: 'I freed your shoulder from the burden; your hands were freed from the load. You called, in distress, and I saved you.'"* – Psalm 81: 7-8. God listens to our cries for help. We became aware that all of a sudden, the Spirit has lifted a heavy load of uncertainty from our chest.

Remember how you survived those moments. Try to remember how you cherished those moments. Always remember that God forgives, saves, guides, embraces, and loves you. Pray to our Lord always that He will help you remember.

In all those moments, in your memories, try to see if God was there or not there.

You may be surprised by a new, greater awareness of God amid your pain or joy. You may find God's love and compassion and draw close to our Lord, whether you are suffering greatly or happily receiving His blessings.

You will realize that God was with you all along. You will find that Jesus was there. Jesus helped you lift the cross from your shoulders, and you got up. You got up. As many times as you fell, you got up. You did.

In the name of the Father, and of the Son, and of the Holy Spirit. Amen.

Prayer: *Lord Jesus, you brought salvation to the human race through your cross. We adore you, and we thank and praise you in faith, joy, and gladness. May your word dwell among us in all its richness. Open our hearts to sing your praises and unceasingly announce your goodness and truth. Guide us and shine your Light upon us so that we may always walk in your path toward the destiny you have set for us. When the final day comes, and we leave this earth, bring us to the radiance of your eternal Light. Amen.*

Notes and References

The Scripture texts used in this work are taken from the Saint Joseph Edition of the *New American Bible*. These texts were chosen for their relevance to my journey and the insights they offer. They serve as a guiding light, illuminating my path and deepening my understanding of my experiences: Catholic Book Publishing Co., New York, NY. 1992. Prayers and scripture texts, as indicated, are also taken from the *Saint Joseph Guide for Christian Prayer (The Liturgy of the Hours)* Catholic Book Publishing Corp., New Jersey, NJ., 1970. *catholicbookpublishing. com;* Catechism of the Catholic Church with Modifications from the Editio Typica. Image Book Doubleday, New York, NY. 1994.

1. T.S, Eliot, *V section, No. 4* of *"Four Quarters"* of *Little Giddings.* Accessed July 18, 2022. *https://www.poetryfoundation.org/poets/t-s-eliot*
2. T.S, Eliot, *V section, No. 4* of *"Four Quarters"* of *Little Giddings.* Accessed July 18, 2022. *https://www.poetryfoundation.org/poets/t-s-eliot*
3. T.S. Eliot. Ibid
4. Accessed June 18, 2022. *https://www.goodreads.com/quotes/68337-the-unread-story-is-not-a-story-it-is-little*
5. See annotation to *John 1:1.*
6. Bible Dictionary, *The New American Bible,* Saint Joseph Edition. New York, NY: Catholic Book Publishing Co.,1992. p. 437.
7. Catechism of the Catholic Church with modifications from the Editio Typica, An Image Book Doubleday, New York, New York 10036. 1994. p. 42.
8. Ibid. p. 43.

9. Most Reverend Oscar Cantu, S.T.D., Bishop of San Jose, CA, Homily at the Opening Mass for the Eucharistic Renewal, June 19, 2022, Feast of the Corpus Christi.

10. Accessed July 28, 2017. https:www//.aleteia.org/2017/07/28/ th-miraculous-story-behind-the-chi-rho-symbol/

11. Ibid.

12. *Shaker of Salt and Flashlight*, Dynamic Preaching, January – March 2017. Margate, NJ: Dynamic Preaching, 2017. Paraphrased.

13. Ibid.

14. Jesus Esplana. *"Fear and Faith"*. *Our Sunday Manna*. Archdiocese of Nueva Caceres, Naga City, Philippines: 2005. p. 83.

15. *Naked and You Clothed Me: Homilies and Reflections for Cycle A*. ed. Deacon Jim Knipper. (Princeton, NJ: Clear Faith Publishing, 2013) p. 235.

16. Deacon Michael Bulson, *Preach What You Believe, Timeless Homilies for Deacons Liturgical Cycle B*. New York, NY: Paulist Press, 2005. p.125.

17. Accessed April 24, 2020. https://en.wikipedia.org/wiki/Stand by Me (Ben E. King song)..

18. Psalm-prayer. *Christian Prayer - The Liturgy of the Hours*. New York, NY. Catholic Book Publishing, 1976. p. 809.

19. I was nine years old at that time (in the mid-1950s; therefore, the catechists most likely were using the 1941 revision of the *Baltimore Catechism*, not the 1885 version). See *The Prophetic Spirit of Catechesis* by Anne Marie Mongoven, O.P., New York/ Mahwah, NJ: Paulist Press, 2000. p. 42.

20. As the Greek word *"catecheo"* means to "echo," I might add that the word "echo" also denotes a sound or something that comes back to its origin once or in a repetitive manner, depending on the location where the echo originates. Echoes are so fascinating to me as they come back mysteriously repeatedly until the sound becomes a whisper, and then disappear entirely.

21. U.S. Conference of Catholic Bishops, *National Directory for Catechesis*, 2005. p. 41.

22. Apostolic Exhortation *Catechisi Tradendae of Pope John Paul II, On Catechesis In Our Time*. 1. https://www.vatican.va/content/

john-paul-ii/en/apost_exhortations/documents/hf_jp-ii_exh_16101979_catechesi-tradendae.html. Supra.

23. Anne Marie Mongoven, O.P. *The Prophetic Spirit of Catechesis*. New York/Mahwah, NJ: Paulist Press, 2000. Ibid. 1.

24. Promoting knowledge of the faith is the first task of catechesis. The other tasks of catechesis are liturgical education/life, moral formation, teaching to pray, belonging to the community, and missionary initiation. (*General Directory for Catechesis*, p. 84-87).

25. U.S. Conference of Catholic Bishops. Ibid. 234.

26. Accessed December 15, 2021. http://www.vatican.va/content/paul-vi/en/apost_exhortations/documents/hf_p-vi_exh_19751208_evangelii-nuntiandi.html.

27. Apostolic Exhortation *Catechisi Tradendae of Pope John Paul II, On Catechesis In Our Time*. Ibid. 5.

28. *Dei Verbum: Dogmatic Constitution on Divine Revelation*. 2. The New American Bible, Saint Joseph Edition. New York, N.Y.: Catholic Book Publishing Co., 1970.

29. *Dei Verbum*. Ibid., 1:2.

30. The Catechetical Documents, *A Parish Resource with Commentary and Index*. Chicago, IL: Liturgy Training Publications, 1996. p.368.

31. Fr. Paul Homes, "*So the last will be first, and the first will be last*" in *Naked and You Clothed Me, Homilies and Reflections for Cycle A*. ed. Jim Knipper. (Princeton New Jersey: Clear Faith Publishing, 2012 p. 253.

32. *A Change of Direction*. Esermons.com. Accessed September 22, 2014.

33. Esermons. Ibid.

34. *Risky Business*, Dynamic Preaching, Vol. XXX, No.4. Oct-Dec 2014. Dynamic Preaching, PO Box 3102 Margate, NJ 08402.

35. *It's Time To Go To Work* by James Merrit. Matthew 25: 14-30. Esermons. Accessed online 6/29/13.

36. *The Compassionate Healings* by Ron Lavin. Esermons.com. Accessed June 24, 2015.

37. Kay Daigle, The Biblical Studies Foundation. https://www. bible. org. Accessed July 8, 2012.

38. *The Legend of Bagger Vance* is a 2000 American sports film directed by Robert Redford, and starring Will Smith, Matt Damon and Charlize Theron. The screenplay by Jeremy Leven is based on Steven Pressfield's 1995 book *The Legend of Bagger Vance: A Novel of Golf and the Game of Life*. The film is set in 1931 Georgia. It was the final film starring Jack Lemmon and Lane Smith. [3]

39. The King's Treasury of Dynamic Preaching Cycles A-B-C King Duncan Resource Publishers. 2014. 327.

    Author's note: This is an excellent preaching guide and is one of my favorite sources for preparing reflections. Some paraphrases were made of sermons or writings including stories other authors selected by Dynamic Preaching. Those writings belong to them or their sources as the case may be. Dynamic Preaching is given due credit. When quoted nothing is taken to imply that they are my own.

    Dynamic Preaching, May-August 2021, Vol. XXXVII, No. 2, p34-36, by King Duncan and Angela Akers, Margate, NY 08402, citing William Barclay in The Parable of Jesus, p. 52. Presbyterian Publishing, Kindle Edition

40. Accessed October 12, 2019. https://en.wikipedia.org/wiki/Risen (2016 film).

41. Accessed August 15, 2020. https://www.usccb.org/offices/general-secretariat/schedule-2015-apostolic-journey-pope-francis-united-states-america.

42. Pope Francis' homily at the Madison Square Garden, New York, U.S.A., September 15, 2015.

43. https://www.patheos.com/blogs/deaconsbench/2014/04/our-servant-pope-wearing-a-deacon-stole-to-wash-feet/

44. Ibid.

45. *Living Faith* by Monsignor Stephen J. Rosetti. Daily Catholic Devotions, January – March 2013. Fenton, MO: Creative Communications for the Parish, 2013.

46. The seven undisputed letters of St. Paul are in the New Testament: Romans, First Corinthians, Second Corinthians, Galatians, Philippians, First Thessalonians, and Philemon.

47. *An Announcement to a Virgin,* Dynamic Preaching. October-December 2014. Margate, NJ: Dynamic Preaching, 2014.

48. *Behold the Lamb,* Dynamic Preaching, January-March 2017. Margate, NJ: Dynamic Preaching, 2017. p.19, 22

49. That is the New International Version (NIV) translation, as well as the New Revised Standard Version (NRSV): "another advocate", translated "like someone who stands beside you in a court of law." The original Greek is *allon parakleton.* Some other translations: King James Version (KJV) – another comforter; Revised Standard Version (RSV) – another counselor; New Common English Bible (NCEB) – another companion. But the literal translation is: one who is called alongside to help. From *Dynamic Preaching.*

50. These words seem to echo Jesus' words in the Gospel. "*I will not leave you orphans; I will come to you.*"

51. Dynamic Preaching, Vol. XXX. No.2. April-June 2014. Ibid.

52. *Happiness Full Stop.* Dynamic Preaching, May-August 2021. Vol. XXXVII, No. 2. Dynamic Preaching. Ibid.

53. Ibid.

54. Ibid.

Printed in the United States
by Baker & Taylor Publisher Services

Printed in the United States
by Baker & Taylor Publisher Services